GERMANY IN THE
GREAT WAR

GERMANY IN THE GREAT WAR

GREAT WAR

Verdun & Somme

Harold Cook

Pen & Sword
MILITARY

AN IMPRINT OF PEN & SWORD BOOKS LTD.
YORKSHIRE – PHILADELPHIA

First published in Great Britain in 2021 by
Pen & Sword MILITARY
An imprint of Pen & Sword Books Ltd
Yorkshire – Philadelphia

A CIP catalogue record for this book is available from the British Library

Typeset by SJmagic DESIGN SERVICES, India
Printed and bound in the UK by CPI Group (UK) Ltd, Croydon, CR0 4YY

Pen & Sword Books Limited incorporates the imprints of Atlas, Archaeology, Aviation, Discovery, Family History, Fiction, History, Maritime, Military, Military Classics, Politics, Select, Transport, True Crime, Air World, Frontline Publishing, Leo Cooper, Remember When, Seaforth Publishing, The Praetorian Press, Wharncliffe Local History, Wharncliffe Transport, Wharncliffe True Crime and White Owl.

For a complete list of Pen & Sword titles please contact
PEN & SWORD BOOKS LIMITED
47 Church Street, Barnsley, South Yorkshire, S70 2AS, England
E-mail: enquiries@pen-and-sword.co.uk • Website: www.pen-and-sword.co.uk
Or
PEN AND SWORD BOOKS
1950 Lawrence Rd, Havertown, PA 19083, USA
E-mail: Uspen-and-sword@casematepublishers.com
Website: www.penandswordbooks.com

Contents

Acknowledgements

Many thanks to Dave Bilton, Ann Coulson and Irene Moore for your continued support. Without you this book would not have been published.

Introduction

This book is the third in a five-part series that documents photographically the exploits of the Central Powers during the First World War. Like previous volumes, this monograph chronicles important aspects of a single year, in this case 1916.

For the Central Powers, it was a year of trial and error, of innovation and drastic changes, with fighting to the west (and the nascent development of *Materialschlacht* or 'attrition warfare'), to the east and further south.[1] For the German Army, 1916 commenced with Operation *Gericht* and the offensive at Verdun. German Chief of the General Staff, Erich von Falkenhayn's stratagem was allegedly intended to 'bleed' the French Army 'to death' (*Blutabzapfung*). And, on the other hand, if the French refused battle, then the 'moral effect' of this 'will be enormous'.[2] Although success was initially forthcoming, victory was elusive, and for approximately 300 days France and Germany were engaged in the 'largest battle of attrition the world had yet seen'.[3]

Seeking to ease the strain on the beleaguered French, Anglo-French forces launched an attack on the Somme, between Gommecourt and Lihons. A combination of 'poor tactics from inexperienced commanders and soldiers, as well as an effective German defence… checked the British assault', resulting in exceptionally high British losses on the first day of the campaign (1 July).[4] Although fighting continued until 18 November, Allied forces made negligible gains, suffering heavily (approximately 420,000 casualties over 140 days) for every metre of ground.[5] The German Army, meanwhile, garnered much from the affair, the campaign demonstrating that 'management' was as important to victory as 'leadership'.[6]

Part of the German Army's difficulties, both at Verdun and on the Somme, stemmed from the poor performance of *Die Fliegertruppe* (the Imperial German Flying Corps). Ineffectual by comparison to the British Royal Flying Corps (RFC) and the French *Aéronautique Militaire*, the Imperial German Flying Corps (IGFC) was unable to gain air superiority.[7] Innovative combined-arms concepts, such as positioning forward observers near the front line, and the establishment of thirty-seven squadrons of single-seater fighters (*Jagdstaffeln*), however, enabled the IGFC to regain ascendancy of the air over the Western Front by the end of the year.[8] Meanwhile, to the east, the situation remained analogous to 1915 with the IGFC unimpeded, capable of providing air-support, over-battlefield reconnaissance and artillery observation.

Verdun demanded additional support on other fronts and coalition forces determined that a second offensive to the East was necessary.[9] Materially inferior and lacking adequate leadership, Russian forces were doomed from the start and an attack at Lake Naroch resulted in approximately 100,000 casualties. German losses were less than a quarter of that figure.

Undeterred, the Russian *Stavka* (High Command) commenced planning a second offensive forthwith. What materialised was a combined-arms offensive along a 32km front against Austro-Hungarian forces in Galicia; one striking 'consecutive blows'.[10] A preliminary bombardment preceded the attack, which began on 4 June. Despite effectively fortified positions, the Austrian Fourth and Seventh armies collapsed under the weight of Russian forces, offering minimal resistance.[11] Only a combined Austro-German offensive succeeded in stalling the advancing Russian armies.[12] The offensive effectively destroyed the Austro-Hungarian Army which suffered the majority of the casualties: approximately 616,000. From then on, the Austrian High Command increasingly relied upon the support of their Teutonic counterparts, the German Army.

Meanwhile, along the border between Turkey and Russia, Ottoman troops endeavoured to frustrate the advance of Russian soldiers at Erzurum, Trabzon and Erzincan. Despite their best efforts and mismanagement of manpower, all three towns were occupied within quick succession.[13] Bitlis, too, was seized, the Russian Caucasus Army overwhelming the Ottoman Second Army after months of heavy fighting.

Meanwhile, in Mesopotamia the besieged remnants of General Charles Townsend's garrison, situated within the town of Kut Al Amara, were struggling to frustrate the onslaught of the Turkish Army. British units, several redeployed from the Western Front, were similarly unable to penetrate the Ottoman front line and after five months of sustained aggression, Townsend surrendered. Kut offered 'brighter prospects for the Turkish Army in Mesopotamia than had hitherto been possible'.[14]

Conditions on the Home Front were less sanguine. A poor harvest, allied with a paucity of transportation, resulted in a winter of stark deprivation for German and Austro-Hungarian civilians. This situation was further exacerbated by the ever-increasing need to relocate food to the front. A system of rationing, designated 'sharing scarcity', was introduced and intended to distribute diminishing foodstuffs. Understandably, resentment was manifest and strikes broke out, resulting in smashed windows, the misappropriation of food and, in some cases, fatalities.[15] Malnourishment was therefore widespread, particularly among senior citizens and the young, leading to complications and other maladies. For example, babies born during the First World War were found to be significantly lighter than was customary.

Privation on the *Heim Front* was a consequence of the 'economic blockade', imposed by Entente maritime forces[16] and the *Kaiserliche Marine's* (Imperial Navy's) failure to frustrate the Royal Navy's blockade.

Across all fronts, whether at home or in Poland, citizens and soldiers alike stood fast against Entente forces. Although success was not forthcoming, a stubborn determination to resist was evident and the Central Powers withstood increasing deprivation on the Home Front and across all fronts.

Chapter 1
Westfront

Today, 1916 is remembered as the year the British Army suffered its worse tragedy in recorded history. At 7.28am on the morning of 1 July, nine corps of the French Sixth Army, along with the British Third and Fourth armies went over the top, from Gommecourt in the north to Montauban in the south. What followed was, in the words of Private E. Houston of the Public Schools Battalion, 'one hundred times worse than any storm'.[1]

Although the word 'Somme' casts a funereal pall over the United Kingdom, its memory is neither universal nor absolute. The campaign is not, as Robin Schäfer argued, 'something that is very much remembered here' in France or Germany. For the men of both the Entente and Central Powers, 1916 was dominated by one of two major campaigns: the battles of the Somme and Verdun (two offensives that in later years came to symbolise, if inaccurately, the supposed futility of the First World War).[2]

The latter campaign (noticeably absent from all but the most comprehensive British histories) commenced on 21 February 1916. Soldiers of the German Fifth Army, following a sustained preliminary bombardment, assailed the French front line surrounding Verdun. Incidentally, the citadel was the last position to fall to German soldiers during the Franco-Prussian War of 1870–71, and was therefore of significant value, both historically and culturally.[3]

The German High Command was well aware of this fact, and anticipated that the French might undoubtedly commit their strategic reserve in order to recapture the position, thereby resulting in heavy casualties through a process of 'attritional warfare'.[4] It was, as General Erich von Falkenhayn surmised, their intention to 'bleed' the French Army 'to death' (*Blutabzapfung*); and if the French refused battle, then the 'moral effect… will be enormous'.[5]

German forces enjoyed initial success, capturing not only Fort Douaumont (the largest and highest fort on the ring of nineteen protecting the city of Verdun), but in reducing French forward divisions by sixty per cent. For example, two French divisions with approximately 26,523 servicemen, were reduced by 23 February to 10,299.[6] Within three days the city and its environs had been razed to the ground and the French army demoralised. Despite holding the initiative, the German High Command failed to monopolise on the situation choosing instead to cautiously probe the enemy defences. As a consequence, by 6 March the advance had slowed considerably, 'developing into the usual prolonged slogging forwards against reinforced defences stiffened with artillery'.[7]

For the next nine months the front line remained relatively static, except for the area between Fleury-devant-Douaumont and Fort Souville, where a salient was driven into the French defences. By mid-December, the belligerents had fought themselves to a standstill. Falkenhayn had underestimated the French, for whom victory at all costs was the only way to justify their sacrifice. In 303 days of fighting, the French Army suffered 377,000 casualties, of whom 162,000 were killed in action (KIA).[8] The German Army was similarly reduced, Robert Foley calculating that losses at Verdun from 21 February to 31 August, were 218,333.[9] Perhaps the most insightful figure is that calculated by Hans Heer and Klaus Nauman, who recorded a monthly average of 70,000, which works out at a daily statistic of 2,333 casualties.[10]

Verdun was, determined John H. Morrow Jr., 'the most terrible battle of attrition (*Materialschlacht*) of the First World War',[11] offering not just the most dreadful conditions that fighting men had ever encountered, but also the most difficult. The unsurpassable quagmire that developed on and around the battlefield (churned up by the pounding of field guns) made movement laborious, slowing advances and restricting the movement of machinery.

Entente forces, seeking to ease the increasing pressure on the beleaguered French, thus launched a limited offensive on the Somme approximately midway through the carnage at Verdun.[12] At 07.28, on the morning of 1 July 1916, Anglo-French soldiers advanced along an 18-mile front.[13]

Although paths through the barbed wire had been cut the night before, traffic jams soon developed and when the German infantry opened fire, concentrating their MG 08 (*Maschinengewehr* 08) on each aperture, British forces were swiftly decimated. Furthermore, allied with the 'terrible' machine-gun fire was, as Private W.H.T. Carter of the 1st Bradford Pals later recalled, the realisation that the British bombardment, which had been estimated to destroy all life, had evidently failed.[14]

However, an impotent preliminary bombardment, scything machine-guns and poor workmanship by the British engineers, were not the main reasons that the offensive was initially ineffectual. Firstly, German divisions on the Somme were an amalgam of regular and reserve regiments and had been stationed in the area since Autumn 1914. They had 'occupied the same sectors for months and knew every feature of the ground intimately'.[15] Secondly, villages lying within or behind German lines were efficiently incorporated into their defences, creating a strong, and in some parts impregnable, trench system. Furthermore, where defences were not fortified by villages, blockhouses were constructed. Frequently located in open country, these sites were selected for their dominance of surrounding ground and became known as redoubts. These fortifications combined to make an excellent defensive position, one that was impenetrable at strategic points for British forces.[16]

It was not all bad news. South of the river the French Sixth Army had achieved significant success, capturing the German front line with comparative ease. The preliminary bombardment had destroyed numerous machine-gun nests and trench mortar pits, while three mines blown simultaneously had further exacerbated any confusion.[17] By 14.00, German forces had been overwhelmed and those who had not been killed or wounded, had fled in panic and 'pulled back hastily to the third position'.[18]

Casualties on 1 July were heavy, for both sides. The British Fourth Army suffered approximately 57,470 casualties, of which 19,240 were killed, while the French Sixth Army endured significantly fewer: 1,590 casualties. The German Second Army meanwhile lost between 10,000–12,000.[19]

Operations on the Somme soon settled into a pattern following the initial assault. Weather permitting, a substantial attack was launched by the Entente every few days, with supporting, flanking operations conducted on either side. Similar to the French, the German Army 'bled copiously under concentrated Allied gunfire – *Trommelfeur* ('drum fire')' – sustaining heavy casualties.[20] The campaign was, in the words of Lieutenant Gerhard Ritter, 'monotonous mutual mass murder'.[21]

Over the next 140 days, Anglo-French forces executed a continuous campaign of smaller operations, slowly forcing the German Army back until poor weather in November precluded any subsequent fighting. Despite commentators arguing that the Battle of the Somme was a profligacy of lives, both sides garnered much from the campaign.[22] For the British it was the beginning of modern combined-arms warfare, with Kitchener's New Army learning to fight an industrial war alongside their coalition partners.[23] For the German Army, the campaign demonstrated that 'management' was as important as 'leadership'.[24]

By December, German casualties across the Somme were approximately 230,000.[25] Combined with losses sustained at Verdun, overall figures amounted to 700,000. Though unsuccessful at Verdun, the German Army had nevertheless weathered the storm of men and machines on the Somme. In fact, the year was instrumental, both from a strategic and tactical perspective, and attritional warfare was now a byword for the ensuing conflict. However, with the advent of inclement weather German forces settled down to a cold winter, awaiting the spring thaw and 'campaigning season'.[26]

German trench, Lorraine. Despite heavy fighting in the region this trench and its surroundings appear untouched. Quiet sectors were not uncommon – fighting was often confined to small areas of the front.

German soldiers collect rainwater that has gathered in shell holes. It is doubtful they will drink it, but use it instead to wash and shave.

Under the watchful eye of a German officer, this soldier starts the long and arduous process of repairing a trench, damaged by shellfire, situated in front of the village of Beaumont-Hamel on the Somme. The officer is a recipient of the Iron Cross.

Sleeping arrangements at the front were often cramped and uncomfortable. These reservists, however, are fortunate to have found a farmhouse behind the front line, which is both warm and dry.

Captured Entente trench. The soldier closest to the camera carries an M1916-issue gas mask case, slung over his right shoulder. The tin was an improvement on the M1915 cloth pouch, which did not protect the mask against both the weather and the rigours of trench life.

French front line trench. The position is littered with military accoutrements including a water bottle, clothing and ammunition.

Holes have been knocked through a French garden wall, thus providing firing slits for the defenders, while the ground in front is strewn with barbed wire.

German forward observer. Note the tangle of barbed wire on top of the breastwork and the corkscrew pickets used to anchor the wire across the front of the trench. The picket was first introduced in 1915 as a replacement for timber posts. They were a silent alternative to the latter and could be screwed into the ground.

German Marine machine gun detachment. Dogs are being used to pull each gun.

Machine gun position, Flanders coast.

German troops, clearly in high spirits, march away from the front line. They will occupy reserve positions for a number of days before returning to the front.

Partially constructed stables.

Stables, constructed by men of *256 Pionier Bataillon*, complete with stalls and even windows. It is doubtful glass has been added, however.

Soldiers enjoy an evening of dancing and singing while billeted in a French village. Even the cooks (dressed all in white) have come out to watch.

Sleeping quarters in a cellar. Such accommodation was much sought after.

Officers' dugout, Western Front. An absence of barbed wire and other obstacles suggests that this particular shelter is either in a reserve or support trench.

German soldiers widen a drainage ditch.

French PoWs captured at the Somme await transportation to the rear and a prisoner of war camp.

These shattered trees are a testament to the awesome power of artillery, whether German, British and French.

The damage caused by artillery was often absolute; a once pretty woodland, situated in northern France, has been reduced to a smattering of stumps following sustained shelling by German guns.

French PoWs, many captured at Verdun, wait to board a train destined for a prison camp somewhere in Germany.

The remains of a village situated in the Vosges Mountains. It is unclear whether the soldier is on guard duty or merely 'sightseeing'. A lack of webbing would suggest the latter.

A 250-metre long 'War Bridge' (*Kriegsbrücke*), France.

A French marketplace (once the centre of the village), is now reduced to rubble.

Telephone exchange located in a forest on the Western Front.

Artillery rounds, fired by German guns, land in and around French trenches close to Chattancourt. The village was the scene of heavy fighting throughout 1916 and witnessed the first use of Diphosgene gas by the Germans on 19 April.

What was once a castle park at Ypres is now a pockmarked wasteland complete with grave markers and shattered trees.

M14 machine gun located on the beach at Flanders. The Maxim Flak M14 was a rapid firing, anti-aircraft weapon capable of firing 37-mm, a copy of the British QF 1-pounder 'pom-pom'.

German trenches under construction.

The road to Forges.

The remains of a French field gun. When in retreat it was common practice among all armies to destroy anything that could be of use to the enemy including arms, supplies and transport.

Belgian PoWs captured defending the Maas River are escorted, under German guard, through a Belgian village.

German soldiers queue to buy food at a stall on the Western Front.

Officers of the German army were often afforded many luxuries while serving at the front including accommodation. This dwelling is situated approximately 600m behind the front line.

German soldiers wearing the newly issued M16 *Stahlhelm* (or steel helmet) march down a French street.

The enemy: British infantry at Guillemont, Somme.

Left: Dugout, Somme. The shelter has been built beneath a house.

Above: German trench under construction.

Below: Market place, Bapaume.

A French village on the Somme.

German trenches, Vermandovillers.

British trenches constructed entirely of sandbags. Given a lack of wood and an excess of soil it seems only natural that such measures were taken.

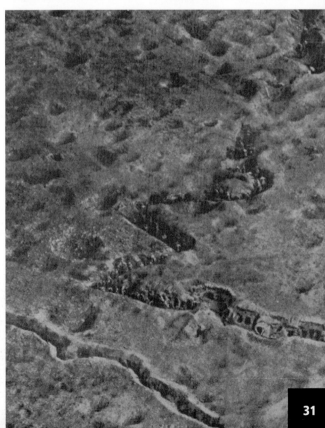

French soldiers, captured on the Somme, are given a meal of coffee and bread by their captors. Both Germans wear the pre-war *pickelhaube*, a spiked helmet made from boiled leather and reinforced with a metal trim.

Canadian infantry somewhere in northern France. Such contemporary photographs highlight the difference in construction between German and British trenches and the reliance on either wood or sandbags.

German soldiers on patrol, Vosges Mountains.

Officers dugout complete with windows, flower boxes and dining table.

German officers survey
the damage caused
by French guns. The
trees surrounding the
position are evidence of
the awesome firepower
of artillery. Both sides
detested long range
shelling, as it was not
only arbitrary, but
also impersonal and
accounted for more than
eighty per cent of all
casualties during the
First World War.

Medical orderlies attend to wounded German soldiers, Vosges Mountains. At least three out of the four wounded have suffered head injuries, either a consequence of overhead shelling or perhaps, as a result of naïve curiosity: it was common among soldiers on both sides to stick their head above the parapet to see the enemy.

General Bruno von Mudra; recipient of the *Pour le Mérite* at his HQ (headquarters) on the Western Front.

German soldiers, equipped with the newly issued M16 *Stahlhelm*, push and pull a field gun into position on the Somme.

Religion was an important part of military life in the early twentieth century; in this photograph, German soldiers attend Sunday mass on a hill in the Vosges Mountains.

Conditions on the Western Front often made movement difficult, for this reason German soldiers construct a road made of railroad sleepers in an effort to beat the foreseeable mud and rain.

British dead.

A cable car in the Vosges Mountains provides not only an easy, but more comfortable, alternative to walking.

French colonial troops captured at Verdun.

German civilians inspect a French aircraft which has crashed in south Germany.

Pionieres (pioneers) of the German army construct a bridge behind the front line. They are attempting, using somewhat primitive tools, to force a tree trunk into the riverbed.

Kaiser Wilhelm and the Crown Prince of Bavaria inspect German troops on the Somme.

Officers of the German army converse with Crown Prince Rupprecht von Bayern, commander of the German Sixth Army on the Western Front. The soldiers, standing to attention, are all recipients of medals awarded for bravery in combat.

Two German soldiers stand amid the ruins of Péronne on the Somme.

A graveyard of automobiles abandoned along the River Somme.

German position, Somme Canal.

French and British prisoners of war, Péronne.

The German Kaiser and Crown Prince visit the Western Front.

The Crown Prince and Prince August Wilhelm of Prussia, accompanied by their aide-de-camp, visit regimental headquarters on the Western Front.

The Grand Duke of Baden, Frederick II, visits a German regiment on the Western Front. Fredrick was the last sovereign of Baden reigning from 1907 until the abolition of the German monarchies in 1918.

Prince Wilhelm of Württemberg visits nurses serving with the German Red Cross on the Western Front.

Officers' quarters.

German field kitchen. Such establishments were often situated well behind the front line. As such, food was often cold or at least tepid by the time it reached those at the front.

German mine shaft. Tunnelling was a response to the deadlock that developed on the Western Front; both sides attempted to undermine the other by digging tunnels packed with explosives.

German forces, in an effort to provide both shelter and accommodation for soldiers serving on the Western Front, excavate and enlarge a dormant French mine.

Map of German trenches on the Somme. The single, black line indicates the position of trenches on 23 June 1916, while the broken and dotted lines denote the extent of the British advance by 6, 20 and 26 July. Péronne is yet to be taken.

German troops on the sea front at Champagne, France.

Soldiers of the French army, now prisoners of war, paraded at Verdun.

German troops in bivouac.

Cavalry patrol, Vosges Mountains.

German munitions column, Vosges Mountains.

Two German soldiers stand in trenches located in woodland on the Western Front.

German trenches situated beneath the ruins of a French farmhouse. It is possible, though it is not clear, that this trench system was originally occupied by French forces, for the French were loath to reinforce or brace their trenches, unlike the Germans.

French food market near Verdun.

Three German soldiers, watched by their peers, fish on the Aisne River.

It was common for soldiers to populate their surroundings with reminders of home, while serving at the front, and these mud huts built by Senegalese soldiers near Verdun highlight this.

Chapter 2
Ostfront

Winter on the Eastern Front passed with only minor activity.[1] The German Army fortified its position, constructing trenches of concrete, equipped with bombproof shelters and light railways and generating plants, from Riga in the north to Ternopol in the south.[2] It was anticipated, due to the constraints of the west, that those to the east should consolidate their position. The territories of Russian-Poland, Lithuania and Latvia were the principal concern, so, too, was the planned German offensive at Verdun.

As such, fighting to the east was largely defensive in reaction to Russian attacks intended to draw German manpower and *matériel* away from Verdun and the ensuing stalemate.[3] Falkenhayn similarly assumed the Russia Army was vanquished, following the Second Masurian Lakes (7–21 February 1915) and the Battle of Gorlice-Tarnow (2 May–27 June 1915), where Russian forces suffered approximately 475,000 casualties, plus 330,000 captured.[4]

Thus, the French appeal for succour, made to Mikhail Alekseyev, Russian Chief of Staff of the General Headquarters, at the beginning of March was therefore unwelcome.[5] The Tsar's army was not strong enough for offensive action nor was it properly equipped. Despite misgivings, the *Stavka* (Russian High Command) was obliged to offer assistance; the Chantilly Conference's mandate dictated that they were required to launch immediate offensive action against the Central Powers to avert subsequent crises.[6]

The campaign opened on 18 March. A two-day bombardment preceded the offensive and was intended to weaken German defences, destroying strongpoints, machine-gun nests and field batteries. Though several thousand tonnes of ordnance was fired, Russian artillery failed to neutralise German defences, the gun layers unable to register their artillery pieces.[7] At 07.00, lead elements of the Russian Second Army, commanded by General V.V. Smirnov, launched their attack at Lake Naroch, 60 miles east of Vilnius (today the capital of Lithuania). A combination of rifle and machine-gun fire, directed by *Generaloberst* Hermann von Eichhorn, met the attackers and as a consequence few survived the crossing. By mid-morning the barbed wire, wrote one German soldier, 'was hung with the corpses of Russian attackers'.[8] Muddy terrain further compounded the offensive, while poor training (the attacking infantry made the mistake of crossing no man's land in small clusters and groups), contributed to the heavy number of casualties.[9]

Though negligible, gains were nonetheless made; the 75th Reserve-Division, south of Lake Naroch, were forced to retire in the face of sustained Russian attacks. Further north the *42 Infanterie-Division*, occupying positions proximate to Postawy, lost possession of their front line. It was only with the arrival of the *107 Infanterie-Division* that the position was retaken the following day.[10]

By 27 March the Russian advance had floundered. General Alexei Evert, commander of the Western Army Group, noted in his report that the offensive had not led to 'decisive results'.[11] Evert blamed the 'onset of warm weather and abundant rains'; the deluge having caused the frozen ground to melt, turning the sector into a quagmire comparable to the Western Front.[12]

The offensive was finally postponed on 30 March. While the German Tenth Army suffered 20,000 casualties, the Russian Second Army lost approximately 80,000 (of which 12,000 suffered or died of hypothermia).[13] According to Norman Stone, Lake Naroch represented, 'the last real effort by the old Russian army… an affair that summed up all that was most wrong with the army'.[14]

In spite of significant setbacks, Russian officers began planning counter offensives almost immediately, their enthusiasm undiminished by their failure.[15] The plan that materialised was presented by General Aleksei Brusilov and proposed a significant offensive against Austro-Hungarian forces in Galicia, along a 250-mile front, striking 'consecutive blows'.[16] Brusilov's plan required surprise and was similarly intended to ease pressure to the west, while monopolising upon the Austro-Hungarian Army's engagement with Italy.

Stavka approved the offensive and Brusilov set about amassing four armies, with a combined force of approximately forty infantry and fifteen cavalry divisions.[17] Incidentally, these forces were initially employed to construct entrenchments along the entire front, thereby providing sufficient shelter, while hindering Austrian aerial observation.[18]

Unbeknownst to the Russians, the Austro-Hungarians had noticed the increased activity. However, buttressed by concrete bunkers and enfilading machine-gun positions, they perceived a fallacious sense of security and invincibility.[19] Conrad, supremely confident, boasted to a Swedish reporter, 'We have held out for two years… We are not to be conquered again'.[20] In essence, argued Holger Herwig, they 'expected Brusilov's attack and were well dug in and prepared to repel it'.[21]

The offensive began on 4 June following a preliminary and merciless hurricane bombardment that decimated the Austrian trench line.[22] Under sustained artillery fire, the Austrian Fourth Army collapsed, offering minimal resistance to Russian forces.[23] To the south, Seventh Army similarly failed to offer more than a token resistance, retiring south, soon followed by the First Army.[24] By the 5th, the situation was incredibly precarious; the Austro-Hungarian position was now under considerable threat. It was only in the centre where minimal progress was made, the German-Austrian *South Army* having impeded Russian troops.

Mass withdrawals followed with Austrian forces retiring along a 250-mile front, stretching from the Pripyat Marshes to the Carpathian Mountains. Many, asserted Jordan and Neiberg, similarly walked towards the Russian lines, 'surrendered as a unit [while others] even switched sides and joined the Russians, believing that the final collapse of the Austro-Hungarian Empire could not be far away'.[25]

Seeking to assuage the Russian onslaught, *Feldmarschall* Conrad appealed to Falkenhayn for support. The German general, however, refused unless all Austrian units stationed in Galicia henceforth operated under German control. Although initially outraged, Conrad capitulated. Falkenhayn thereafter dispatched three divisions from the Western Front.[26] This culminated in a combined Austro-German offensive seven days later that succeeded in stalling the Russian offensive.[27] Allied with this was the fact that their initial and impressive gains had come as something of a shock to the Russians. 'Tail' units (or logistical organisations) had not yet drawn level with their 'teeth' (combatant units). Thus, surrounded on all sides, *matériel* soon diminished, making it problematic to continue.

Though costly, the Russian offensive diverted substantial elements of the Central Powers away from the Western Front to the east. In total, eighteen German divisions were transferred from the west, thereby frustrating the offensive thrust of the German Army.[28] The Brusilov Campaign further crippled the Austro-Hungarian Empire, which suffered the majority of all casualties: approximately 616,000. From then on, the Austrians increasingly relied upon the support of their counterparts, the German Army.

Professor Tunstall argued that it was 'the worst crisis of World War I for Austria-Hungary and the Triple Entente's great victory'.[29] Norman Stone, meanwhile, declared it 'the most brilliant victory of the war'.[30] This appears, however, somewhat of an exaggeration. The campaign is now regarded as a limited strategical success, simultaneously saving Italy, while diverting considerable German reserves from Verdun to the east, thereby relieving pressure on the French Army.[31] Yet for the Central Powers, and despite the loss of momentum within France, there was much to be grateful for. Control of Austro-Hungarian forces was a considerable coup, providing the Germans with effective control of subsequent operations on the Eastern Front.

Thus, 1916 ended as it had begun. Although Russian forces had inflicted significant damage upon the Austro-Hungarian Army, while limiting the fighting capacity of the Central Powers, they had failed to weaken the German Army. Now in complete control of the situation, the High Command began planning for offensives during 1917. Furthermore, victory for the Russians came at a price. With over 2 million casualties, the Tsarist Army was effectively demoralised.[32] As a result, more than a dozen regiments mutinied in December; one company even sending a telegraph to the Tsar declaring, 'Take us and have us shot, but we just are not going to fight any more'.[33] 1917 therefore looked promising for the Central Powers.

Austro-Hungarian trenches, Eastern Front. The position is not only well fortified, but also heavily defended with at least two machine guns situated behind sniper plates.

To combat both aerial observation and the strafing of trenches by enemy aircraft, a machine gun has been situated along the trench line.

Members of the Austro-Hungarian Red Cross carry wounded soldiers down a communication trench. Considering not only the weight of the individual, but also the terrain and width of the trench, it is an impressive feat.

German soldiers sit 'chatting' (a common practice in which soldiers sat in groups systematically destroying body lice, while conversing between themselves), in a crater caused by a Russian mine.

An Austro-Hungarian grenadier prepares to throw a Model 14 *Zeitzünderhandgranate* (hand grenade) at a Russian trench on the Eastern Front. The photograph is clearly staged, for the fuse, situated on top of the grooved cast iron cylinder, is unlit.

In the general melee of trench warfare, it was not uncommon to find unorthodox weaponry rubbing shoulders with the conventional. Here Punji sticks (wood spikes) have been inserted into the ground and barbed wire wrapped around each stake.

Field battery and telephone exchange.

German armoured field gun.

Generalleutnant Hermann Clausius (right).

General Friedrich von Bernhardi (centre). He fought with success first on the Eastern Front and then to the west.

Generalmajor Wonna (right) and Professor Donnstedt. The difference in bearing, despite both wearing uniform, is striking.

Lice were a problem on all fronts. In this photograph, Russian PoWs prepare to enter a delousing shed.

Serbian PoWs.

Conditions on the Eastern front were frigid and desperate and prisoners on both sides fought the elements. In this picture a group of Serbian soldiers march towards a prisoner of war camp.

German officers, clad in overcoats and wearing scarves, are escorted to the rear under Russian guard.

Though forbidden on the Western Front, it was common practice to use enemy soldiers as stretcher-bearers to the east. These Russian prisoners have been given the difficult task of carrying Austrian wounded down the side of a mountain in Montenegro.

German forces intern all Serbian men of military-age.

Russian PoWs on the Eastern front. Their living conditions are surprisingly good considering they are prisoners of war.

German working party.

Field post office.

It is unclear whether these two individuals are merely curious or are paying their respects; prudence would suggest the latter.

Letters sent from home, yet to be sorted, lie on the ground outside a German field post office.

Russian soldiers, now prisoners of war, await transportation to a German camp situated well behind the front line.

Soldiers in retreat often set fire to towns and villages; by torching such settlements retiring forces effectively denied the enemy both shelter and resources.

German soldiers watch from the side of a lake as a Russian village burns in the distance. Many still wear the infamous German *pickelhaube*; they are yet to receive the M16 *Stahlhelm*.

The gutted and charred remains of a factory at Brest-Litovsk.

Russian casemates, Eastern Front. Barbed wire supports have been dumped unceremoniously in front of each.

The effects of sustained bombardment on Russian fortifications.

Austro-Hungarian camp (*lager*). Chairs and other home comforts, stolen from villages en route to the front line, make life slightly more bearable.

Captured Russian siege howitzer.

Storage dump.

German soldiers inspect a captured Russian caisson (a two-wheeled cart designed to carry artillery ammunition).

The remains of a railway bridge over the Neman River, Belarus.

Soldiers disassemble a captured Japanese 28cm Howitzer L/10 employed by Russian forces.

Russian siege cannon, now operated by soldiers of the German army.

Captured Russian fortress.

German soldiers take a minute to marvel at a bridge destroyed by Russian forces retiring in the wake of their advance.

Three German soldiers stand amid a shell-hole created by a 42cm shell.

Fort VII, Poland. Constructed during the early 1880s the fortress was a part of the defence of Warsaw. It was captured in 1914 and remained in German hands until 1918.

Fort VIII, Warsaw. A complex of apartments now surrounds the fortress.

Two examples of the Russian-made PM M1910. The Model 1910 was a water-cooled, heavy machine gun chambered for the standard Russian 7.62 x 54mm rifle cartridge.

Jews, citizens of Poland, are photographed as part of a mandatory identification process for all nationals.

A woman accused of spying for the enemy is tried by a military court of law.

A public notice hung between two houses reads, 'Soldiers! Take care! In this village is cholera!'

A monitoring station for those infected with cholera. Today the disease is largely dormant, yet during the early twentieth century it ran rampant through most of Europe.

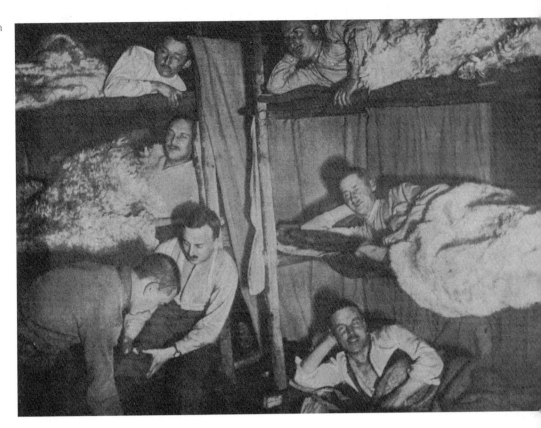

German dugout, Eastern Front. Each soldier has been issued with a sheepskin blanket.

Dressed all in white, a patrol of German soldiers fire their rifles at targets in the distance.

Officers' quarters.

German trenches, Eastern Front. Heavy rains and a lack of proper drainage have turned the position into a veritable lake.

Engineers build shelters behind the front line intended for use by German soldiers in reserve.

Catholic field mass and Holy Communion.

Religious ceremonies were common on all fronts and all denominations were represented. In this photograph an Evangelical pastor holds a service for men serving at the front.

German trenches on the Eastern Front.

Dugout, complete with flower patch and shrubbery, wooden fences and even a letterbox.

Horse-drawn rail cars.

Engineers lay a series of barbed wire entanglements on the Eastern Front. They are using wood stakes rather than corkscrew pickets, which had by 1915 replaced the former.

Austro-Hungarian engineers construct a temporary road somewhere in Poland.

An Austrian *Feldjäger* (field hunter) battalion bivouacs for the night; rifles staked in groups of four.

In order to impede the passage of enemy soldiers, gates covered with barbed wire were erected at strategic points. Each gate could be lowered at a word of command, thus checking the progress of the enemy, while forcing him to either fight his way through or climb up and out of the trench.

German shelter, Eastern Front.

The drainage of water was an issue on all fronts; here, two German soldiers attempt to excavate a drainage channel in a trench on the Eastern Front.

German field gun.

Looking towards the Russian front line.

To the reader such a scene as the one pictured may appear macabre. Yet for those serving, death was commonplace, the dead merely an indication of success or failure.

German trenches near Potsdam.

Trenches on all fronts were in a constant state of repair; here engineers fell trees to be used as braces and supports in a trench system on the Eastern Front.

Russian PoWs under German supervision collect wicker baskets used to carry field artillery shells.

General Hermann von Eichhorn greets soldiers serving on the Eastern Front. Eichhorn was considered a superb military tactician, commanding the Tenth Army from 21 January 1915 until 5 March 1918 when he was appointed supreme commander of Army Group Kiev and military governor of Ukraine.

Austro-Hungarian artillerymen prepare to fire a field gun from beneath an improvised wicker canopy.

Russian prisoners, now serving as stretcher-bearers, carry a wounded soldier to the nearest aid station.

The other end of the spectrum: an Austro-Hungarian trench on the Eastern Front, bereft of all but the bare essentials.

German field kitchen.

Russian PoWs serve as part of a transport column in Galicia. Such practices were common on all fronts.

German field hospital. Pine needles have been used not only to cover the roof, but also decorate the outside.

Artillery observation post.

German cavalry, closely followed by a field kitchen (foreground), ford a stream on the Eastern Front. A temporary road has been constructed by laying planks of wood side-by-side.

German soldiers, many carrying mattocks and shovels, march past a village on the Eastern Front. It is unclear whether they are entering or exiting the front line. Clean clothing would suggest the former.

A Russian field battery somewhere near Dünaburg (today Daugavplis, Latvia).

Russian shelters.

German soldiers resting. It is possible that this is a forward sap: a shell crater that has been enlarged and is then used as a listening post.

Sunday afternoon in the trenches.

Austro-Hungarian column.

Austrian soldiers advance through Albania. The country was occupied until 1918, when a multi-national Allied force broke through the Austro-Hungarian and German lines.

Artillery positions overlooking Durazzo (modern day Durrës, Albania).

German soldiers bathing in the Barda River (Perm Krai, Russia).

Bulgarian troops eat lunch beside a river in Macedonia.

Austrian forces commandeer provisions intended for a Montenegrin village, including *zigaretten* (cigarettes).

Away from the front line, Austro-Hungarian soldiers take a moment to relax. They are seated on beer barrels waiting on a quayside in Montenegro.

A Bulgarian officer inspects horses under the care of farmers, now serving in the Bulgarian army.

German field hospital, Macedonia. A mix of Austro-Hungarian, Bulgarian and German soldiers are seated around the trestle tables.

The citizens of Monastir (Bitola, Macedonia) celebrate the birthday of Ferdinand I of Bulgaria. Ferdinand was the ruling prince of Bulgaria from 1887-1908 and later Tsar from 1908-18.

Austrian soldiers collect water from a well in east Galicia.

Field gun battery.

Austro-Hungarian infantry fire at Russian positions on the Eastern Front.

Bombproof shelter.

Austro-Hungarian machine gunners prepare to fire a *Maschinegewehr* (*Schwarzlose*) M7. The *Schwarzlose* MG was a water-cooled, belt-fed machine gun typically mounted on a tripod.

Chapter 3
Gebirgskrieg

On the Italian Front (or *Gebirgskrieg*, 'Mountain War'), both sides spent the winter undercover, endeavouring to weather the frigid freezing temperatures of the Dolomites. For Austro-Hungarian and Italian servicemen, this was their first time in the 'frozen Alps'.[1] Many were understandably impatient, anxiously awaiting the spring thaws, yet simultaneously dreading the 'campaigning season'.[2]

The year opened with a bang, when Austro-Hungarian engineers detonated a 300lb mine at Lagazuoi. Conventional attacks involving masses of infantry and Alpine personnel had proven ineffectual. Fortified entrenchments, reams of barbed wire, machine guns and artillery had 'removed all possibility of manoeuvre'.[3] The Austrian High Command was therefore keen to circumvent the Italian front line. Tunnelling offered a means of bypassing and outmanoeuvring the enemy, while reducing further casualties and forcing 'the landscape to work in their favour'.[4]

Despite their best efforts, the mine 'exploded too far from its target to cause any damage'.[5] Yet, the attack nonetheless had a demoralising effect on Italian forces. With no experience of 'mining', they were notably shaken. However, no further action was taken and both sides settled down, once again, to an otherwise undisturbed existence, punctuated by sporadic bouts of small, insular fighting.

Then on 9 March, Italian forces launched an offensive across the Isonzo (Soča) River, the scene of four previous campaigns.[6] Part of the Chantilly Agreement, the attack was intended to divert German and Austro-Hungarian manpower away from Verdun and the preparations at Lake Naroch.[7] After a week of heavy fighting, 'snow in the north and fog in the south forced a cessation'.[8] The attack had been inconclusive, with Italian gains limited to Mount Sabatino. Austro-Hungarian counter offensives had similarly frustrated further attempts and the Italian Army retired unceremoniously. Rather blithely, success had been anticipated simply because of a superiority in men and *matériel*. Furthermore, so misguided and outdated was the Marshal of Italy Luigi Cadorna's understanding of attritional warfare that no systematic fighting doctrine was implemented.[9]

Skirmishes continued until 30 March, in a protracted struggle for ascendancy of the region. However, no subsequent offensives were conducted and by mid-April fighting had ceased. The Austrian Official War History (or, *Oesterreich-Ungarns letzter Krieg, 1914–1918*) rather derisively dismissed the campaign, designating it as 'an attempt by the enemy to pretend there had been a serious battle'.[10] Mercifully, casualties were not exceptionally high: 1,882 Italian and 1,895 Austrian dead and wounded.[11]

Defeating Serbia in November 1915 enabled the Austro-Hungarian High Command to redistribute troops from the east to the Italian Front. Similarly, reinforcements meant that the Hapsburg Empire might exact revenge for the Italian refusal to join the Triple Alliance the previous year. Enraged by the enemy's betrayal, *Feldmarschall* Conrad von Hötzendorf had conceived of an ambitious plan to punish them; a cunning offensive titled 'The Battle of Asiago' and nicknamed the *Strafexpedition* (or 'punitive expedition'). Germany strongly disagreed with the plan and when asked to provide support demurred.[12]

Undeterred, Conrad persisted with his preparations, amassing 1,200 field guns plus 260 battalions over the course of three weeks: an approximately fifty per cent increase.[13] On 15 May the offensive was launched and resulted in immediate tactical success, with Austro-Hungarian forces advancing 12 miles. Nevertheless, owing to the impossibility of moving artillery across the mountainous terrain, the Austrians were unable to capitalise upon the situation and the *Strafexpedition* soon ground to a halt.

To make matters worse, on 4 June the dramatic and unexpected Brusilov Offensive was launched, necessitating the transfer of significant Austrian reinforcements. The situation was further exacerbated by the Italian Army who reinforced the line, effectively frustrating any subsequent advances. Thus, the *Strafexpedition* was abandoned six days later. Italian casualties were between 140–150,000, including 40,000 prisoners taken during the initial phase, while the Austro-Hungarians suffered approximately 80,000. Overall, the campaign was one of the bloodiest and yet most unsuccessful of the war, Austro-Hungarian forces vacating the captured positions.[14] In fact, although the attack succeeded in breaking the Italian front and penetrating some of the northern Italian plains, these gains were not retained.[15]

Flushed with victory, the Italian High Command began planning another campaign. Frustrating the Austrian offensive had, argued Schindler, 'vastly improved the morale of the Italian Army and nation', and a sixth attack was therefore initiated along the banks of the Isonzo River.[16] The objective was Gorizia, a small, rural town in north-eastern Italy, and many thus referred to the coming offensive as the 'Battle of Gorizia'.[17]

The attack opened with an intense bombardment by 1,200 artillery pieces (450 of them being medium and heavy guns) on 6 August, resulting in the destruction of reinforced trenches, dugouts, ammunition dumps, machine-gun posts and Austro-Hungarian artillery positions.[18] After incredibly costly hand-to-hand fighting, and without the withering retaliatory fire so common, Italian forces seized Mount Sabotino and San Michele, along with the main transport line. This enabled the advance upon Gorizia.

Approximately 51,221 Italians were killed, wounded or missing against 37,458 Austrian casualties.[19] Furthermore, the Austrian's lost an 'important and threatening bridgehead and a dominating position on the Carso'.[20] In Italy, the offensive was deemed 'the first authentic... victory of the war'.[21] So successful was the attack that two subsequent campaigns were undertaken, to monopolise upon the situation, although neither achieved comparable success to the sixth.

By the end of the year, both sides were exhausted, following the series of recurrent and lengthy campaigns. However, the year was not yet over. Avalanches were a frequent occurrence among the mountains, and on 12 December several struck Italian and Austro-Hungarian positions, killing an estimated 10,000 within a month.[22] Many were the result of artillery shells and resultant explosions. Others were of course natural, considering the time of year and the increase in snowfall.[23]

The Italian Front of 1916, similar to other theatres, was symptomatic of the 'fundamental characteristic of modern war – lengthy battles of attrition which consumed men and munitions… without winning much ground'.[24] Though partial gains were achieved, significant casualties made such advantages negligible. Overall, the Austro-Hungarian Army ended the year in a far better position than it had started, despite numerous setbacks and the failure of the *Strafexpedition*. Although other fronts had demanded significant reinforcements, thereby resulting in fewer servicemen, occupying the high ground limited casualties, enabling the Austrians to hold the line. Thus, 1916 was a year of varying successes.

Italian prisoners of war. Most, but not all wear the standard issue steel helmet, a licensed version of the French M15 Adrian helmet first introduced in 1915.

Austrian wounded stand-at-ease in a village on the Isonzo Front.

Officers of the Austro-Hungarian army examine an Italian biplane which has crashed in a field of crops. The damage is so extensive that it is difficult to tell that this was ever an aeroplane.

Austro-Hungarian observation post. The trench runs parallel to the Isonzo River, which can be seen in the background. This particular section of the line is considered the end point or *der endpunkt* of the front line.

Alpine troops.

Austro-Hungarian soldiers, Tyrol Front. Both are equipped with white smocks and hats.

The defender often had the advantage of high ground. Here Austro-Hungarian troops snipe at Italian forces high in the Tyrolean mountains.

In the absence of horses and even donkeys, dogs were used to pull and carry heavy equipment, weaponry and personnel.

Above: 'How do we look?'

Left: A bombproof telephone exchange on the southwest front.

Opposite: Due to the nature of the terrain, tunnelling and other forms of excavation on the Italian Front were onerous and labour intensive. In this photograph, Austro-Hungarian miners use pneumatic drills to cut bombproof shelters into the mountainside.

The Central Powers, unlike the Entente, were known for the construction of their trenches. This particular trench is located on the Southwest Front.

Austro-Hungarian telephone exchange, Dolomites. An observer has been posted in order to keep a look out.

The entrance to a bombproof 'foxhole' (*ein Fuchsloch*).

Austro-Hungarian soldiers pose next to a captured Italian 15cm field gun.

Another bombproof shelter. Not only have steps been hewn out of the rock, but handrails and makeshift sheds constructed.

Repairing a broken telephone line.

Wounded Austrian soldiers are carried down the mountains and away from the front line.

Russian PoWs carry a wounded Austrian soldier down the side of a mountain in the Alps.

Italian fort, Monte Verena. This particular fortification witnessed heavy fighting and was captured by Austrian forces in April 1916.

Austro-Hungarian front line, Isonzo Front. The position is most likely close to or next to the Isonzo River. It was a natural barrier and a source of drinking water.

Italian gun emplacements, Monte Verena.

Alpine troops scale a ridge in the Dolomites.

Austro-Hungarian patrol.

Supply train, somewhere in the vicinity of the 'Three Peaks'.

Outpost dogs (*borposten-hunde*).

Radio and communications technology was still in its infancy during the First World War. Here an Austrian NCO reports back to base from a patrol he is leading in the Italian Alps.

Fighting on the Italian Front was often highly mobile. In this photograph an Austro-Hungarian patrol, having reached high ground, prepare to ambush enemy forces.

Austro-Hungarian mountain field gun battery.

A Maltese hospital situated on the Tirol Front. The roof has been covered with foliage, a counter measure against observation from the air.

Austro-Hungarian sap, Alps.

Searchlights were used in a variety of different roles including, aircraft observation and as a preventative measure against enemy attacks on land and at sea.

Underground shelter, complete with field kitchen.

Italian prisoners of war, Isonzo Front.

Austro-Hungarian camp (*lager*).

Though the terrain was mountainous, wooded and at points impassable it was, if nothing else, beautiful.

Machine gun detachment, South Tyrol. The men are clearly not in danger from small arms fire for the commander has exposed himself above the parapet.

The border village.

Austrian machine gunners hide in the rubble of a house on the Isonzo Front.

Feldmarschall Karl Franz Josef, commander of the XX Corps (Edelweiss Corps), led his troops during the South Tyrol offensive in the spring of 1916.

In trench warfare it was not always possible to avoid naturally occurring obstacles. In this photograph, an Italian trench cuts directly across a tributary on the Isonzo Front.

Feldmarschall Karl Franz Josef inspects troops of an Austro-Hungarian machine-gun detachment.

Side street, Burgen (Borgo).

Italian
prisoners
march through
a town in
south Tyrol.

12cm *Minenwerfer* M15 (trench mortar) emplacement; foliage covers the gun preventing observation from the air.

The church of St Matteo prior to the Battle of Asiago. The town was almost completely destroyed during the war and its demise featured in the poetry of Ernest Hemingway.

Above: Fort Lisser was built between 1911 and 1912 and was part of a series of fortifications designed to dominate and protect the inhabited town of Enego. The fort itself witnessed heavy fighting and as a consequence was moderately damaged.

Left: Ospedaletto train station.

Below: Aircraft, such as this Italian monoplane, were considered by many to be a marvel of modern technology and so attracted large crowds who came to gawp at such machinery.

Field guns, unless properly emplaced with either timber or concrete beneath, tended to sink dramatically after each shot.

Soldiers of the K.u.K *Radfahrer-Seebataillons* (cyclist marine battalion).

Austro-Hungarian naval gun, Adria.

First aid post established after heavy fighting on the Bessarabian Front.

Austro-Hungarian field kitchen located high in a cave in the Alps.

The gutted remains of a factory on the Eastern Front.

Chapter 4
Türkei

By 9 January the last remaining Anglo-French servicemen had evacuated the Gallipoli Peninsula. Although fighting had taken a devastating toll on the Ottoman Army, they were nevertheless victorious. Under the command of General Otto Liman von Sanders, Ottoman forces had effectively impeded Entente endeavours to seize the Dardanelle Straits, therein enabling them to besiege Constantinople (Istanbul), and secure a warm water port and supply route to Russia.[1]

Attention thus turned to other theatres. The Ottoman Army was divided between multiple regions, including Sinai, Mesopotamia, the Caucasus, Galicia and Macedonia.[2] The division of labour and resources was causing serious logistical problems and it was anticipated that reinforcements from Gallipoli might bolster other sectors.[3]

The first events of the year occurred in Iraq when British forces made several attempts to relieve the besieged garrison of General Townsend. However, with 'three entrenched positions… bloody fighting' ensued, the Turks withstanding each attack, effectively repulsing British infantry divisions despatched from the Western Front, while engendering considerable casualties.[4] Though some died where they had fallen, many were pronounced dead en route to Basra. Medical services, anticipating only minor casualties, had established facilities for 250 wounded servicemen. With ten times that number resources were stretched and many of the wounded were forced to subsist for days without water on the banks of the Tigris.

Ottoman forces were under the command of *Generalfeldmarschall* Colmar Freiherr von der Goltz, a hard-nosed, ruthless individual who had established a reputation as military governor of Belgium throughout 1914.[5] In fact, the high-ranking officer was so callous that his exploits were commended by Adolf Hitler who remarked, 'the old Reich knew… how to act with firmness in the occupied areas'.[6]

Over the course of the following months, several subsequent attempts were made to relieve the beleaguered garrison. However, on 29 April the remnants of Townsend's depleted force surrendered, following a protracted siege lasting five months. It was a stunning victory and one that Christopher Catherwood contends was the 'worst defeat of the Allies in World War I'.[7] Goltz never lived to witness 'the victorious outcome' of his campaign, dying of spotted typhus on 9 April.[8] Recent scholarship has calculated that British losses, from December 1915 to April 1916, were approximately 23,000 either killed in action (KIA), wounded in action (WIA) or captured.[9]

Further west, a considerable expeditionary force was developing with a campaign planned against the Suez Canal in February.[10] Various factors, however, militated against its initial execution. It was therefore not until July that an Ottoman-German raid was conducted, involving the 3rd Turkish Division, together with contingents of German and Austrian artillery units, machine-gun companies and one aviation squadron,[11] a combined total of approximately 12,000 servicemen.[12] While the raid achieved the element of surprise, success was limited and by 7

August, Third Army had retired, following a counterattack by British reserves that had 'hammered' the Turks.[13]

Manoeuvre warfare continued across the Sinai and Palestinian Front throughout the year and by December numerous, smaller campaigns had been conducted, pushing Ottoman forces back towards Gaza. Transportation was a critical factor throughout the campaign. While the Turks relied predominantly on camels and oxen for logistical support, the Egyptian Expeditionary Force (EEF) were reliant on railways and pipelines.[14] However, their failure to construct adequate supply lines severely hampered their ability to advance, especially when waterholes and other sources of water were destroyed.

Meanwhile in Persia, Ottoman forces launched a second invasion, undertaken by XIII Corps with approximately 25,000 troops. Though artillery support was promised by the Germans, it was not forthcoming and the offensive soon floundered. Von Sanders determined in his memoirs *Five Years in Turkey*, that the advance was 'from a military point of view a great mistake'.[15] The *Generalleutnant* argued that the offensive should never have started until British forces had been evicted from Iraq.

On other fronts, Ottoman forces were engaged in a brutal campaign against the Russian Army in the Caucasus. Frequently dwarfed by the successes of 1915 at Gallipoli, the Turkish Third Army was fighting a war of defence (despite initially seeking the offensive in 1914), both to regain significant territorial losses and divert Russian troops from the Eastern Front.[16]

Winter is often a time of resupply, of husbanding resources and preparing for the coming spring months and warmer weather. However, Tsarist forces, aware of how ill-prepared the Ottoman Army was, following the devastating losses at Gallipoli and, conscious that those available servicemen might 'reinforce the Caucasian Front...from early spring', mounted a surprise offensive on 10 January.[17] Over eight days, the Turks were besieged, eventually retiring in the face of the sustained onslaught. Several factors contributed to their failure, including, most notably, a lack of reserves to stem the Russian breakthrough.[18] Third Army losses were exceptionally high, with 20,000 killed, wounded or captured. This was out of 65,000 soldiers that the Third Army had started the battle with: nearly one-third of its overall strength.[19]

In March, following a succession of subsequent setbacks and after losing ground, the Ottoman Third Army was again assailed, this time at Bitlis: a small, strategically-important fortified town near Moush and a stronghold on the fringes of the Empire. A blizzard obscured advancing enemy forces, surprising the defenders. Intense hand-to-hand combat ensued and after several hours of sustained fighting, the Turks fled south, retiring in the direction of Siirt and abandoning twenty field guns and approximately 1,000 servicemen.[20]

Although Bitlis was initially lost, it was recaptured later in the year, following a successful Ottoman counter-offensive in August directed by Mustafa Kemal (Atatürk). The senior officer rallied his troops, despite serious issues of morale.[21] His success, declared Allen and Muratoff, was due to 'the attached auxiliary formations, mobile and familiar with the ground, that proved useful out of all proportion to their numbers'.[22]

In light of his limited success, Kemal was charged with organising the defence of the region. However, Ottoman forces were too weak and poorly equipped to mount significant opposition and by November had retired further into Anatolia, following a series of failed offensives. The rest of the year was spent reorganising and drastically revising their strategic objectives, for the Turkish commanders appeared incapable of appreciating 'the direction of attack which could promise the most favourable results'.[23] Furthermore, with approximately 30,000 killed or wounded, the effective fighting strength of the Ottoman Third Army was reduced by over one third.[24]

Nevertheless, 1916 proved to be, as Edward Erickson demonstrated, 'the high tide of the Turkish Army... It was a year of triumph and of defeat as the Turks attempted to regain the strategic initiative that they had lost.'[25] By the end of the year, the Ottoman Army was engaged across multiple fronts, fighting the Russians, French, together with British and Commonwealth forces. Although support, both monetarily and *matériel* was appearing from Germany, it was nonetheless incredibly slow because of 'strategic transportation deficiencies'.[26] Furthermore, 'fruitless' offensives in the Caucasus, remonstrated von Saunders, allied with significant losses (in personnel), demonstrated that the Ottoman Army was still teething.[27] However, though Ottoman forces were struggling, the year had proven that they were nonetheless capable of weathering any storm.

Turkish engineers carry logs towards the front line, Caucasus.

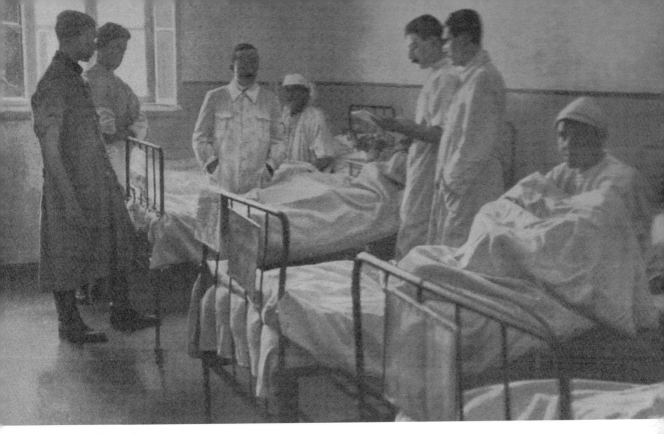

Turkish hospital, Jerusalem.

Syrian locals watch as a column of Turkish infantry passes on its way to a troop show at Damascus.

Turkish officers.

Officers of the German medical corps are photographed standing in front of a Turkish hospital sharing a hookah pipe with a local Iman.

After a day's heavy marching, a detachment of Turkish *Landstrum* makes camp.

Turkish PoWs.

Persian militia, Tehran.

Middle-aged Turkish men, all reservists, answer their country's call.

Water in any environment is a precious commodity; Turkish infantry stop at a watering hole to replenish their supply of the lifesaving liquid.

Ottoman bivouac, Syria. The assorted mix of rifles and sabres indicates that these soldiers are cavalrymen of the Turkish army.

The Shah of Persia, Ahmed Mirza is photographed (second from the left) standing next to a Russian biplane.

Arab elders meet with German officials.

A Turkish field battery fords a river in Mesopotamia. They are equipped with the German-built 15cm sFH 13 howitzers.

Turkish supply train.

It was important, despite personal grievances, to keep up appearances. For this reason, German officers meet with Bedouin chieftains.

Turkish troops, Taurus Mountains.

As the largest humanitarian organisation in Turkey, it was the Red Crescents' responsibility to provide medical support to those wounded on the battlefield. In this photograph, staff members pack their equipment in preparation for the front.

Camel caravan.

A column of Entente soldiers, under Turkish guard, marches away from the front line and into captivity.

Lieutenant Hans Klein, German aviator and air ace (credited with twenty-two confirmed kills), is photographed with Ottoman dignitaries and soldiers following a successful flight across Egypt and the Suez Canal.

The key to a successful campaign is improvisation. In this photograph, horses pull rail cars along a stretch of railroad in the Sinai desert.

Disease was rampant in the desert. Camels of the Ottoman army convey pharmaceutical supplies to the front.

German hospital (right) situated on the main raid to El Arish.

To be effective, an army relies on large amounts of food. Thus, gathering the harvest was just as important as fighting the enemy.

The Galata Bridge, Constantinople (modern day Istanbul).

Austro-Hungarian awards ceremony, Constantinople.

Arab locals use cylindrical rafts to carry their cargo of watermelons down the Tigris.

German-made trucks cross a river via wooden rafts, Mesopotamia.

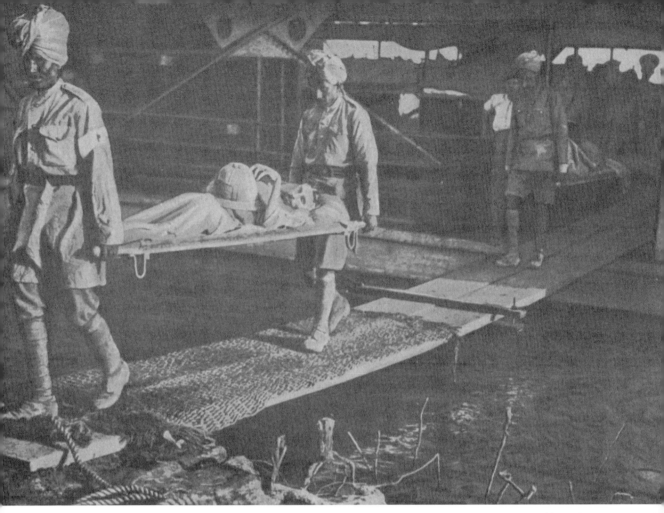

Skeletal Indian soldiers, many severely malnourished, are carried ashore from a hospital ship. These lucky few are the survivors of General Townshend's beleaguered garrison at Kut-al-Amara.

General Townshend, Commander of the British garrison at Kut-al-Amara, is photographed being driven through the streets of Constantinople.

British PoWs captured at the Suez Canal.

Turkish soldiers, under German supervision, wheel field guns aboard a boat anchored at the port of Constantinople.

Turkish sFH 13 (15cm *Schweres Feldhaubitze* m/13 L/17 Howitzer) battery. A direct hit is clearly considered unlikely given the proximity of the ammunition to the field gun.

A Turkish camel transport column, Syria.

Oxen of the Austro-Hungarian army pull a battery of field guns across the Syrian Desert.

German citizens, many of them young children, are photographed next to a camel, a present from their ally to the south: Turkey.

City Park, Karlsruhe.

Turkish and German soldiers drive nails into a memorial cannon on the Bajazid Square.

Generalfeldmarschall August von Mackensen, Constantinople. Mackensen was responsible for a multi-national army fighting on the Eastern Front.

Owing to a lack of motorised transport, camels were often used as vehicles. This creature is employed as an ambulance.

Chapter 5
Die Fliegertruppe

1916 was the first year that serious air campaigns were conducted by either side. Aerial warfare, especially air combat, was nascent, although burgeoning. It had been recognised that 'control of the air was the prerequisite for the effective employment of air power'.[1] Both the Entente and Central Powers endeavoured to gain ascendancy of the air, developing faster aeroplanes, with impressive manoeuvrability and increasing rates of climb.[2]

One element of these developments, however, was to transform aerial warfare. The 'synchronisation gear' or 'gun synchroniser' was under development in France and Germany prior to the outbreak of hostilities. This simple, yet effective mechanism, permitted airmen to fire machine guns, of varying calibres, through the arc of a spinning propeller: a revolutionary component, considering the variety of weaponry, including 'pistols, shotguns, and rifles and even... bricks and grenades' that had been employed, prior to its establishment.[3] Though under development in France, the Imperial German Flying Corps (IGFC) was the first organisation to introduce the device, securing the appliance to the Fokker E.I (essentially an armed version of the Fokker M.5K single-seat reconnaissance aircraft) in mid-1915.[4] Incidentally, the IGFC anticipated that the synchronisation gear might enable German airmen to gain supremacy of the air, thus rendering Allied access to vital intelligence (derived predominantly from aerial reconnaissance) extremely dangerous to acquire.[5]

Such a stratagem was therefore envisaged at Verdun, the IGFC assembling several hundred fighters to expedite aerial ascendancy, therein enabling observation balloons and aircraft freedom of movement, while simultaneously denying French efforts. Elements of these units were known as *Kampfeinsitzer Kommando* (or KEK). These single-seater battle units were comprised entirely of fighter-only aeroplanes and designed to simply destroy French aircraft and observation balloons. The *Aéronautique Militaire*, however, responded, declared Mahoney and Pugh, 'with a concentration of fighter units whose sole purpose was to operate in combat air patrols searching out German aeroplanes'.[6] Organised by Major Charles de Tricornot de Rose, this consortium of French machines soon dominated the skies over Verdun. 'The mission of the escadrilles', maintained the senior commander on 2 March, 'is to seek out the enemy, to fight him and to destroy him.'[7]

Thus, air ascendancy was slowly wrested from the Germans, forcing the IGFC to turn their attention away from attacking French aeroplanes and towards protecting their own. By August, 'French fighters had regained control of the skies above Verdun.'[8] With the bulk of their forces concentrated opposite Verdun, the Anglo-French onslaught on 1 July took the IGFC by surprise. Thus began, in the words of the German High Command, the 'blackest days in the history of

German war aviation'.[9] General Fritz von Below, commander of the Second Army similarly declared, 'the enemy's aircraft inspired our troops with a feeling of defencelessness'.[10]

French doctrine at Verdun had shaped the Royal Flying Corps' approach and conduct in the air, and British airmen swiftly dominated the airspace, keeping German fighters and reconnaissance aeroplanes out of the skies over the Somme.[11] However, as the fighting around Verdun diminished, the Germans transferred all available aircraft south. By August, approximately sixty single-seat fighters were stationed on the Somme and by mid-October this had increased to 540: two-thirds of the IGFC.[12]

To the east, fighting was enacted on a much smaller scale. The geographic scope of the Eastern Front made comparable combat missions more challenging. Reconnaissance, instead, became a central tenet of the campaign and was most notable during the Brusilov Offensive, when German aircraft dominated the Galician skies 'little hindered'.[13] Like Verdun, the IGFC denied the enemy air supremacy and thus the acquisition of vital intelligence. Such tactics were understandably deleterious to the Russians. As Major General Sir Alfred Knox, liaison officer to the Imperial Russian Army observed, referring to the Brusilov Campaign, 'The [Russian] artillery has been hopelessly handicapped by the lack of aerial observation.'[14]

Aircraft were similarly employed to strafe columns of infantry and cavalry, with both sides undertaking *strafen* ('punishment') missions.[15] Such operations were often highly effective, given the tight proximity of the marching servicemen and the lack of cover on roads and other tracks. In a single pass, one aircraft might inflict twenty or thirty casualties, within a matter of seconds.[16]

In other theatres, similar developments were transpiring. For example, in Palestine the Prussian air squadron FA 300 was dispatched to eliminate Commonwealth ground targets, undertaking a combination of *strafen* missions and bombing campaigns.[17] Operating alongside the IGFC was the Ottoman 'Air Force' (a gross exaggeration, given both the size and structure of the organisation), whose personnel were stationed across various theatres, including the Mesopotamian, Caucasian and Sinai fronts. Whereas air operations during 1914 and '15 were 'sporadic', contributing 'little to the overall ground war', by early-1916 the situation was changing, for both the Ottomans and IGFC.[18] A slow, but steady stream of aircraft (sent by the German High Command) had enabled the Turks to amass approximately ninety machines[19] that were operated by men, proclaimed David Nicolle, 'from the Turkish heartland... others came from the Arab provinces of the Ottoman Empire as far south as Yemen, or even from neutral Iran'.[20]

Their numbers were augmented by German *Fliegerabteilung* detachments that began arriving from the start of the year. Despite their numerical inferiority, these aircraft retained air supremacy in Palestine and Sinai, conducting a variety of operations, including attacking British forces situated in Mesopotamia. On 1 March, three German aircraft bombed the besieged garrison of Kut; a paucity of AA (or anti-aircraft) guns, however, frustrated retaliatory action and there were no casualties. This was, as Major General Charles Townsend recorded, incredibly fortuitous. 'If any of the German pilots had fallen into the hands of my troops he would have been torn to pieces… as the victims were often women and children and our poor wounded in the hospital.'[21]

Aerial combat was not confined to the front line. The *Heim Front* was equally susceptible to attack and was considered a soft target. Following an unexpected (and phenomenally devastating) raid on Karlsruhe conducted on 22 June, Germany began organising a home defence command, thereby improving the coordination of 'vital elements of the country's air defence system'.[22] The Karlsruhe raid therefore marked, argued Geinitz, 'the further totalization of warfare in the air'.[23]

The High Command was keen that similar operations should not be repeated.[24] Attacks against civilians were both an embarrassment and deleterious to morale. Thus, the localised air defences comprised single-seater fighter units and flak positions, situated at strategic points within Germany.

There was also a need to take the fight to the enemy. The first raid of the year against the British homeland was conducted by the *Kaiserliche Marine* (or Imperial German Navy). Nine Zeppelins bombed the environs of Liverpool on 31 January to 1 February. Approximately 61 people were killed and 101 injured, reported *The Times* four days later.[25] Miraculously (and owing to the inclement weather), all but one Zeppelin returned, L19 landing in the North Sea due to engine failure. Although the crew of sixteen survived the initial splashdown, the failure of a British fishing trawler, *King Stephen*, to rescue them led to their deaths. The incident sparked coverage worldwide, with the German government and some elements of the British press, condemning the actions of the trawler's skipper, William Martin. Others, including Arthur Winnington-Ingram, the Bishop of London, praised Martin for placing the safety of his crew foremost.[26]

Raids continued throughout 1916. London, Hull, Sevenoaks and Swanley were all bombed, killing hundreds and destroying thousands of pounds worth of property. Over the course of the year, twenty-three raids were conducted, 100 tons of ordnance dropped and approximately 300 British civilians killed and countless injured.

Though aerial warfare was nascent in 1916, the year demonstrated two important details. Firstly, aerial observation was paramount, German doctrine reflecting that in 'positional warfare… aerial spotting takes on a decisive role within the whole context of the battle plan'.[27] Secondly, 'the side that possessed the best aircraft momentarily commanded the sky.'[28] Aeroplanes, such as the Fokker F.I and Albatros D.III, dominated the skies over the Western Front, their rate of climb and manoeuvrability overshadowing the Entente machines.[29] Furthermore, although aerial ascendancy was lost following Verdun, the IGFC and ancillary air forces nonetheless enjoyed considerable success across other theatres. For example, Austro-Hungarian and German aviators dominated the skies over the Eastern Front and throughout Sinai and Palestine. Thus, 1916 was, for the IGFC (which as of October 1916 was re-designated *Der Deutsche Luftstreitkräfte*), a year of introspection, and while ascendancy was as yet forthcoming, it was undoubtedly merely a matter of months before it was again wrested from the enemy.

Above: A village in Eastern Europe burns after being struck by ordnance dropped by an Austro-Hungarian flyer.

Opposite above: Georges Guynemer, the French air ace, is photographed seated in his Nieuport 10. A sesquiplane (one-and-a-half wings), the Nieuport entered service in 1915 and was used in a variety of different roles including, as a fighter, trainer and reconnaissance aircraft.

Opposite below: German soldiers inspect a Vickers F.B.5 (the 'Gunbus') shot down by German fighters over Lille. The pilot has clearly made an attempt at landing his aircraft but has tipped forward as a consequence of the uneven ground.

A German aviator, piloting an Albatros C.III (a two-seater general-purpose biplane), circles high above a French ammunition train destined for Verdun.

It was common practice, certainly among allies, to lease equipment for use to other countries. The aircraft in this photograph is a French Voisin III bomber, which was bought by the Russian government and has subsequently crashed on the Eastern Front.

An Italian ('Double Decker') Caproni Ca.3 shot down over the capital of Slovenia by Austro-Hungarian aviators.

Leutnant Gottfried Freiherr von Banfield prior to take off. Banfield was the most successful Austro-Hungarian naval pilot of the First World War, with a total of nine confirmed and eleven unconfirmed air-kills.

A Zeppelin P Class airship, LZ-48 (L.15), photographed off the English coast following an air raid over England.

Dover train station, as pictured from 3000m.

After crash landing in the sea a French pilot is rescued by the crew of a German floatplane. The aircraft is a Friedrichshafen FF.29 a lightweight, two-seater biplane capable of landing on water.

The skeletal remains of *LZ-59* (L.20), a Q-Class Zeppelin. It was the first of its kind to be built and carried out a total of nineteen flights, including two raids on England before it was forced to land on 3 May 1916, due to engine failure.

With fields far below and forests stretching as far as the eye can see, a German aviator is pictured piloting an Albatros B.II.

Captured enemy aircraft were routinely examined. In this photograph, three officers, presumably pilots, study a British Vickers F.B.5.

A group of German pilots stand discussing a captured Caudron G.4, a twin-engined biplane, widely used by the French for bombing.

German Albatros C.I prior to take-off. The rear cockpit is fitted with a ring-mounted 7.92 mm *Parabellum* MG14. This particular model has a rectangular rather than cylindrical sight and a drum magazine.

Above: A German pilot is carried ashore by a mechanic.

Left: *Kapitanleutnant* (Captain) Joachim Breithaupt, the commander of *LZ-48* (*L-15*). Breithaupt was captured on 1 April 1916, and this photograph was taken while in captivity.

Below: What looks to be a rescue party is in fact, a clandestine rendezvous: a naval officer aboard a German U-boat passes important documents, captured on the high seas, to a German pilot on the wing of a Friedrichshafen FF.33 floatplane.

Chapter 6
Kaiserliche Marine

The *Skagerrakschlacht* or Battle of Jutland, fought between the 31 May and 1 June, entirely dominates the British and German naval historiographies of the First World War[1] – and for good reason. It was the largest, most significant naval engagement of the war, culminating in the defeat of the Royal Navy and the rather extraordinary success of the Imperial German Navy. This was not the only offensive action undertaken by the German Navy that year. However, the psychological impact was nonetheless manifold.

Despite this, the primary objective of the engagement was never achieved. The German High Seas Fleet (GHSF) was numerically inferior to the British Grand Fleet (BGF). The intention of the GHSF therefore was to adopt a stratagem of 'divide-and-conquer'. First compel the British Grand Fleet to depart Scapa Flow, then surround, isolate and eventually destroy them. Unfortunately for the GHSF, their plan was intercepted by the Admiralty, who garnered, via signal intercepts, that a major fleet operation was imminent and therefore encouraged Admiral of the Fleet John Rushworth Jellicoe, to set sail in pursuit. 'Urgent', declared the Admiralty signal, 'There are indications that German fleet are in outer roads by 7pm tonight and may go to sea tomorrow'.[2]

Nevertheless, our story begins on the morning of 31 May, off the coast of the Isle of May.[3] SM *U-32*, while on patrol, sighted two light cruisers, HMS *Galatea and Phaeton*, exiting the estuary.[4] Both were destined for Scapa Flow, located in the Orkney Islands and home to the British Grand Fleet.

At a range of approximately 1,000m, *U-32* fired the first, and only torpedo, at the two cruisers. HMS *Galatea* turned, while *Phaeton* manoeuvred towards the submarine attempting to ram it.[5] In an act of self-preservation, *Kapitänleutnant* Kurt Hartwig, commander of SM *U-32*, ordered the crew to crash dive (a manoeuvre in which the submarine submerges rapidly, thereby avoiding a sudden attack). On ascending to periscope depth ten minutes later, Hartwig observed the cruisers steaming southeast. Too far away to pursue, the commander of SM *U-32* nonetheless reported the sighting to the German Admiralty: 'two large battleships, two cruisers, several torpedo boats... heading southeast'.[6]

Later that afternoon, *Galatea* and *Phaeton*, operating as part of the 1st Light Cruiser Squadron, encountered two German destroyers, SM *B109* and *B110*. Both parties had been investigating the presence of a neutral Danish steamer, *N J Fjord*, bobbing lifeless in the North Sea.[7] The RN cruisers opened fire first, their initial volley of shot, however, fell wide and the German destroyers withdrew. They were swiftly replaced by elements of *Konteradmiral* (KAdm)

Friedrich Boedicker's 2nd Scouting Group. Pitched, running engagements erupted and at 14.36, SMS *Elbing* struck *Galatea*, a single shot landing on the deck.[8]

Further north, Vice Admiral David Beatty, commander of the 1st Battle Cruiser Squadron (1/BCS), received notification of the developing encounter. Beatty had garnered this information from signal intercepts. Manoeuvring southeast and then eastwards, the squadron began steaming towards the German High Seas Fleet. The 5th Battle Squadron, however, missed Beatty's initial change of course.[9] Thus, the four battleships and one battle cruiser were soon approximately 8.7 nautical miles behind the 1/BCS.[10] (This blunder was to prove fatal, subsequently costing the Royal Navy an overwhelming advantage, both in ships and firepower during the first half-hour of the engagement.)

Beatty aimed to intercept *Vizeadmiral* (VAdm) Franz Ritter von Hipper. The latter had other ideas, however, endeavouring to draw the 1st and 2nd Battle Squadrons out, thus enabling *Admiral* (Adm) Reinhard Scheer, Commander-in-Chief of the German High Seas Fleet, to ambush the two. At 15.22, and at a range of 13 nautical miles, Hipper's forces sighted elements of the British Grand Fleet, turning southeast towards Scheer. Forty minutes later and with the British Grand Fleet parallel, Hipper opened fire.[11] The 1st and 2nd Battle Squadrons, however, were slow to react and were still manoeuvring as the first salvo crashed out. Undeterred, Beatty responded in kind. Yet, neither side scored any hits.

What followed next has been termed the 'Run to the South' and involved VAdm Hipper leading Beatty's 1st and 2nd Battle Cruiser Squadrons towards Adm Scheer, waiting further south. After this came the 'Run to the North' and then the 'Night Action'. By 05.20 on 1 June, the battle was effectively over, with the German High Seas Fleet and British Grand Fleet steaming towards port. SMS *Ostfriesland* was the final casualty, striking a British naval mine. One man was killed, a further ten wounded.[12] Total losses on both sides were 9,823. The German High Seas Fleet suffered approximately 3,039 casualties, while the Royal Navy lost 6,784 killed, 674 wounded and 177 captured.

At noon the following day, the German government issued a press statement. Victory, the communication determined, had been achieved and the German High Seas Fleet, for the loss of two craft (SMS *Pommern* and *Wiesbaden*), had sunk fourteen enemy ships, including HMS *Black Prince, Invincible* and *Tipperary*, together with the Acasta-class destroyers *Nestor* and *Shark*. News concerning the destruction of four more German craft was withheld, however; such information was unknown to the enemy. The announcement, made by Adm Eduard von Capelle to the *Reichstag* on 3 June, was similarly published in the *Daily Mirror*. 'The result of the fighting', declared the Secretary for State of the *Reichsmarineamt* (Imperial Naval Office), 'is a significant success for our forces against a much stronger adversary'.[13]

The British populace were shocked. The Royal Navy, undefeated for 300 years, the nation's 'shield', had received a significant blow.[14] If the RN was unable to maintain a presence in the open waters surrounding the British Isles, how were they to defend against invasion or, more importantly, impose economic sanctions? The RN High Command, ever diplomatic however, cautioned against defeatist talk and, in a speech to the British Imperial Council of Commerce (BICC) on 8 June, Arthur Balfour, First Lord of the Admiralty maintained, that 'if any man seriously entertained the view that invasion was possible, did he not now regard it one of the many unfulfilled dreams which the war has dissipated for ever [sic]?'[15]

Though the Battle of Jutland was among the 'greatest naval battles of all times', argued Epkenhans et al, its impact was more psychological rather than material.[16] Despite suffering significantly greater losses, both in men and *matériel*, control of the North Sea and the passage of goods remained in the hands of the Royal Navy. As one newspaper reasoned, 'will the flag-waving German people get any more of the cooper, rubber and cotton their government so sorely needs? Not by a pound. Will meat and butter be cheaper in Berlin? Not by a pfennig. There is one test, and only one, of victory. Who held the field of battle at the end of the fight?'[17]

Thus, wary of the British Grand Fleet, the German High Seas Fleet conducted only two more sorties into the North Sea, following the Battle of Jutland. While the latter occurred during the spring of 1918, the former was undertaken a few months later, between 26–27 October. German torpedo boats (*Torpedoboot*) launched an attack under cover of darkness on the straits of Dover, endeavouring to disrupt the Dover Barrage: an underwater blockade 'comprising deep and shallow minefields' intended to inhibit the ingress and egress of German U-boats into the English Channel.[18] Eight British craft, including HMS *Flirt*, three destroyers, three drifters (essentially tugs or commercial fishing trawlers) and the troop transport *Queen*, were sunk.

Lieutenant R.P. Kellett, commander of *Flirt*, had, upon challenging the unidentified craft, withheld his fire; the approaching vessels having responded to his identification request with the correct password. Kellett therefore, rather naturally assumed, that they were friendly. Overall, forty-five RN sailors were killed, four wounded and ten captured. Meanwhile, German losses were slight, SMS *G-91* suffering minor damage.[19] Stimulated by their unparalleled success, the German High Command commenced planning subsequent missions, both within the North Sea and English Channel. However, none were carried out. Nonetheless, the raid demonstrated, at least to the British Admiralty, that the Dover Barrage was 'largely ineffective'.[20]

For the Imperial German Navy, 1916 was a mixed bag. Despite the psychological impact of Jutland and their success across the Dover Barrage, their High Seas Fleet was unable to combat the economic blockade. Failure to wrest ascendancy of the seas from the Royal Navy further exacerbated conditions at home, disadvantaging German and Austro-Hungarian citizens and their attendant armies. Furthermore, although the German fleet had theoretically triumphed at the *Skagerrakschlacht*, their failure to augment their success meant a nominal rather than material victory. 'Give or take a few insignificant military raids on the English east coast', the GHSF was confined to the North Sea.[21]

A German warship fires a salvo out to sea.

Sailors of the Imperial German navy scrub the deck of a warship while at sea.

A torpedo is loaded aboard a German warship.

Sunday service.

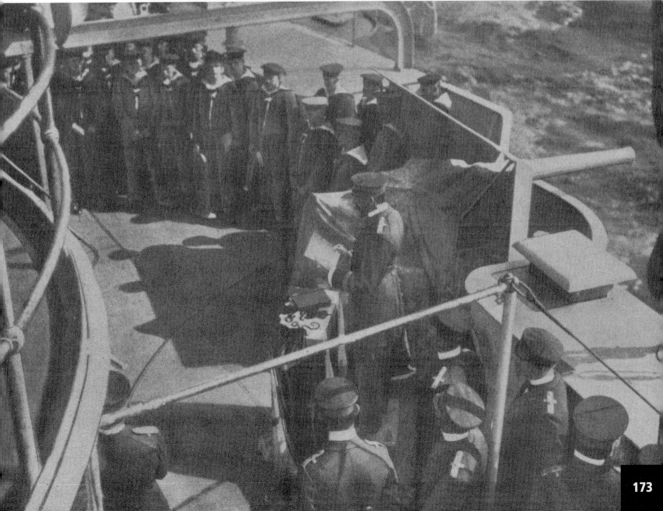

German Dreadnought battleship.

German sailors clean the barrel of a 21cm SK L/40 (*Schnelladekanone Länge 40*) naval gun.

German sailors pose for a photograph in Yeniköy, a neighbourhood in the Sariyer district of Constantinople (Istanbul).

U-boats were reliant on a 'mother-ship' when at sea. These vessels provided basic necessities such as food, water, fuel and ammunition.

U-Boot-Mutterschiff ('U-boat mother ship').

A German submarine sets sail.

A German submarine surfaces alongside another U-boat, in order to transfer tinned produce and other *matériel*.

Torpedo room, German U-boat (*Unterseebootes*).

Quick firing cannon (*schnellfeuercanone*) aboard a German U-boat.

In addition to a cargo of bombs, a single carrier pigeon is placed aboard a German seaplane. In case of emergency, pilots were advised to release the bird with a message attached detailing their location.

Seamen aboard a German submarine fire a deck gun at an unseen target.

Engine room, German U-boat.

Repair begins on a German cargo steamer damaged by a British torpedo.

A French steamer slowly sinks, her cargo rising to the surface following an attack by SM *U-35*. The barrels are doubtless filled with produce destined for the front.

The officers of SM *U-35*. From left to right, Lieutenant Terra, Captain von Arnauld de la Perière, Engineer Göhrs and Lieutenant Lonke.

SS *Sussex* photographed at Boulogne, France, following an attack by SM *UB-29* on 24 March 1916. The entire bow forward to the bridge has been blown off.

Bon Voyage. German seamen wave goodbye to loved ones onshore.

A German seaman 'accidentally' sloshes seawater over three unsuspecting shipmates, enjoying the view aboard a German submarine.

Two German U-boats, one of them SM *U-35*, meet in open water in order to exchange information.

Commander Nikolaus zu Dohna-Schlodien, German naval officer and author, addresses the crew of SMS *Möwe*. Dohna-Schlodien, along with his men, achieved great success during the First World War sinking numerous vessels, including SS *Georgic*.

Prisoners aboard the merchant raider, SMS *Möwe*.

German sailors are photographed off the Portuguese island of Madeira prior to the German declaration of war in March 1916.

Chapter 7
Heim Front

Writing in 1938, Hans Fallada, German novelist and author of *Little Man, What Now,* documented his experiences during the First World War. Unfit for active service, Fallada remained at home and detailed the steady decline of life on the *Heim Front*.[1]

By January 1916, the German populace, although accustomed to war and its limitations, were effectively starving, the British naval blockade having frustrated the delivery of all imported goods which Germany relied so heavily upon. Products such as tobacco, meat, beer, soap and even cabbage, taken for granted in peacetime, were now not just in short supply, but considered a luxury. As a consequence, their value had risen and by 1916 most had increased in price by one hundred and fifty per cent since the start of the war.

As inflation increased, so too did rationing. First introduced in 1915 as a measure of austerity, rationing was initially confined only to the basics. By 1916, however, the list had increased to include all items considered 'non-essential'. To begin with, rationing worked fairly well; each citizen over the age of 18 was issued a ration book. Inside was a series of coupons, each coupon roughly the size of a postage stamp, and on it was printed the item of food, its weight in grams, and the province in which the individual was entitled to redeem it.[2] Allowances, dependent on circumstance, were accorded however; women in the last three months of pregnancy received extra rations, including full milk, to which children under the age of six were also entitled. While workmen undertaking critical or hard labour, essential to the war effort, were entitled to 600 grams of bread daily and a double ration of potatoes.[3]

Though it spread the sacrifice evenly and ensured the well-being of all, rationing was greeted with a mixture of anger and suspicion. Citizens in Germany and Austro-Hungary resented the restriction of food. Rioting thus increased from the previous year, while acts of vandalism and theft were manifold. In May and again in September, German women and children protesting bread shortages not only broke windows, but pillaged the interiors of local shops.[4] In late July rioters, aggrieved by the discovery of large quantities of potatoes found rotting in warehouses, looted the contents of local bakeries, smashing windows and goods counters. An unexpected increase in the harvest that year had meant that not all the potatoes could be delivered.

Episodes of violence were perhaps an understandable reaction to the crises, given the restrictive diet. Limited in nutritional value, many found themselves not only malnourished, but susceptible to disease and infection. Maladies such as rickets, tuberculosis, parasites, influenza, lung infections and pneumonia, diseases of the circulatory system, diphtheria, typhus, dysentery and diseases of the urinary and reproductive organs were rife.[5] Civilians, far from being mere auxiliaries, were now targets in war, the economic blockade by the Entente having blurred the line between the combatant and non-combatant.[6]

Malnourishment was most acute in new-borns and infants. Three-year-old children born in 1914 were found to be on average 2.5lbs lighter than was normal for their age. This was approximately seven to ten per cent of their total body weight. Furthermore, a study conducted in 1919 comparing 300 children from Berlin in 1908–09 with children of the same age in 1919, found that the growth of boys and girls had been retarded by between one and a quarter and one and a half years.[7] Women, too, suffered disproportionately, and the additional five million involved in some form of war work had to cope with increasingly arduous domestic responsibilities allied with hard labour. Thus, 'the reduction in diet, together with the increased physical and psychological stress often proved fatal'.[8]

Good news was on the horizon, however. With the occupation of Rumania in late August, Germany seized 54,000 rail cars of grain and a further 1,000 of crude oil per day. This was in addition to 170,000 head of cattle, 190,000 sheep, 50,000 hogs and 50,000 turtles per annum, plus 6,000 freight cars of grain, 14,000 of potatoes, 3,000 of coal, 1.9 million eggs, and finally, 1.7 cubic yards of wood per day from Albania, Poland and Serbia. Yet, with a population of 62,272,185 this equated to 0.0002 potatoes, 0.00004 pieces of coal, 0.03 eggs, 0.002 per cent of a single cow, 0.003 per cent of a single ram and 0.0008 of a pig or turtle.[9]

As the year progressed, it slowly became harder to obtain food. Throughout the war, Ann Kohnstern, a resident of Hamburg, wrote letters to her son Albert, serving on the Western Front. Her correspondence offers a glimpse into the world of the German civilian at *Heim*, and dwells upon the lengthy queues of between 600 and 800 people that frequently formed outside varying establishments. In April she wrote, 'shopping for food is becoming ever worse. One is underway the entire day and still gets nothing.'[10]

Terms quickly emerged concerning the procurement of food, including the word 'polonaise'. This was used to describe the sensation of shivering, which frequently occurred while waiting in line, especially during the winter months.[11]

Family members, too, often worked together to survive. Whereas food had previously been sent to the front, from 1916 onwards this was reversed. Soldiers in occupied countries, with an expendable income and sufficient nourishment, bought items for their families at home. This offset, but did not frustrate, starvation.

'Total war' similarly meant that there was more to consider than servicemen at the front, and an influx of Russian prisoners of war (or PoWs), together with thousands of refugees entering Lower Austria and its capital, Vienna (Hungary refused to host them), made it still harder to acquire food.[12] On top of this, the wounded needed feeding too, there were approximately 260,000 injured servicemen at 306 makeshift Austrian hospitals.[13]

For the civilians of the Central Powers, 1916 was, in the words of Alexander Watson, 'grim'.[14] Further measures of austerity, allied with disappointments at Verdun and the Somme, and the ever-growing list of casualties across all fronts, increased manifest feelings of despondency. Hopes of a quick victory had faded and the year was a mixture of exhaustion, impoverishment and anxiety. Further suffering was on the horizon, too, for the winter of 1916–17 was to be the worst in living memory, resulting in a poor harvest and appellation, the *Streckrübenwinter* (or 'Turnip Winter').[15] 1916 on the *Heim Front* was defined primarily by sacrifice.

Members of the National Women's
League of Berlin-Wilmersdorf collect
pumpkin and cherry kernels.

Rheinstein Castle, opposite the vineyard
of Assmannshausen.

Soldiers stationed in Poland gather leaves for the front. Foliage was often used for kindling, bedding as camouflage.

German mechanics dismantle a Vickers FB5 shot down by German flying ace, Captain Boelcke.

German soldiers and French civilians enjoy a Sunday concert in a public park, Lille.

Delegates of military societies from across Germany mourn the death of Captain Boelcke killed on 28 October 1916. Mentor to flying ace, Manfred von Richthofen (The Red Baron), Boelcke was one of the most influential practitioners of air combat during the early years of the First World War. Boelcke's grieving mother is photographed at the top.

Scenes from inside a German slaughterhouse. This series of photographs captures the process of manufacturing tinned goods containing meat.

German youths, many hoping to one day join the German army, take part in an endurance race organised by the Crown Prince, Wilhelm II.

German cooks prepare a lunchtime meal for wounded soldiers aboard a hospital train.

Interior view of a hospital train for wounded German soldiers.

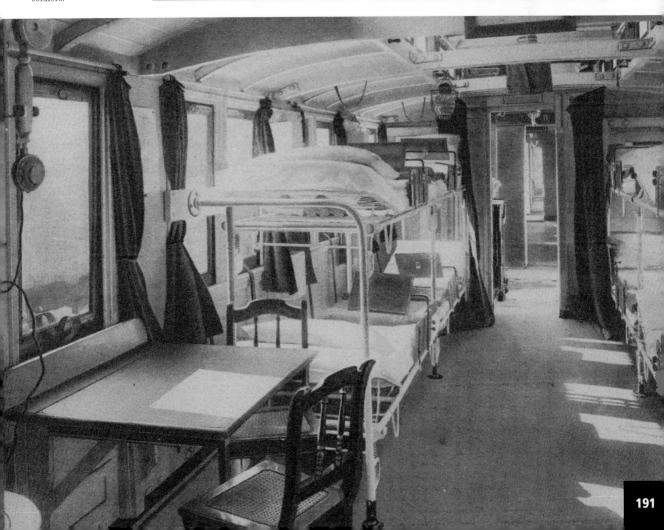

Above: German infantry practise scaling obstacles, while carrying haversack and rifle. Some have chosen to ignore orders, however, and circumvent the fence skirting around it to the left.

Left: Peter Kopp killed on 16 November 1916, Rumania.

Below: German postcard celebrating the birthday of King Wilhelm II of Württemberg. He ruled from 1891 until the abolition of the kingdom in 1918.

German women operate machinery designed to form percussion caps for rifle cartridges.

Athletic contests were organised throughout Germany on a yearly basis and featured a range of sporting activities, including the high jump.

193

Somewhat of an unusual sporting activity by modern standards: grenade throwing.

A 3000m team race.

One unlucky competitor has fallen over while attempting to ford the water jump (part of a steeplechase organised by the German army).

German officials look on as a French prisoner of war paints a picture of what one can only assume is his sweetheart or wife.

Prisoner of war camp, Stuttgart. Inmates are encouraged to take up recreational activities such as sculpture.

Peeling potatoes at a war kitchen in Mannheim.

War kitchen wagons prepare to distribute food to those suffering as a consequence of the British economic blockade.

Cutting cabbages.

Machine washing potatoes.

War wounded, some without arms or legs, practise digging.

War wounded, amputees, assorted civilians and German soldiers pose for the camera. This is a staged demonstration of how modern prostheses might aid those who have lost limbs in tasks such as the cutting of crops.

German cavalry.

War wounded,
all missing legs,
manufacture prosthetic
limbs.

Limbless German
soldiers practise
operating machinery
in the Orthopaedic
Hospital School
at Hanover. It was
anticipated that these
men could be employed
in factories across
Germany once they had
mastered the use of
their prostheses.

French PoWs, captured at Verdun and now interned in Germany, practise boxing as a recreational pastime.

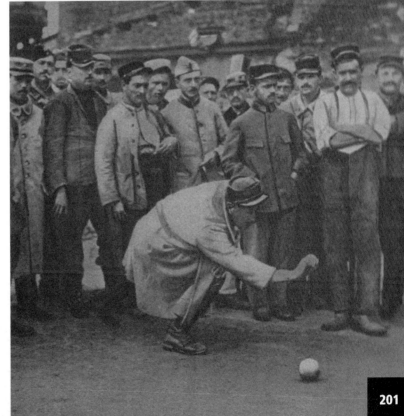

Boules, a game in which the objective is to throw or roll heavy balls as close as possible to a smaller target ball, is played by French PoWs at a camp outside Stuttgart.

Belgian rabbits.

Exhibition of rabbits raised by military bodies, Berlin.

Angling on the River Somme.

German soldiers, convalescing at Davos, enjoy an afternoon sleigh ride.

Wounded German infantry arrive at the recreational home in Switzerland.

German wounded and civilians watch a bobsleigh race, Davos.

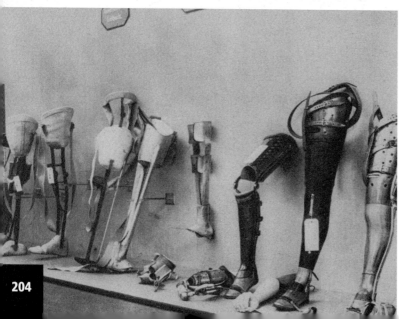

Artificial arms and limbs.

Operating room on the *Auguste Viktoria* (Augustus Victoria) hospital train.

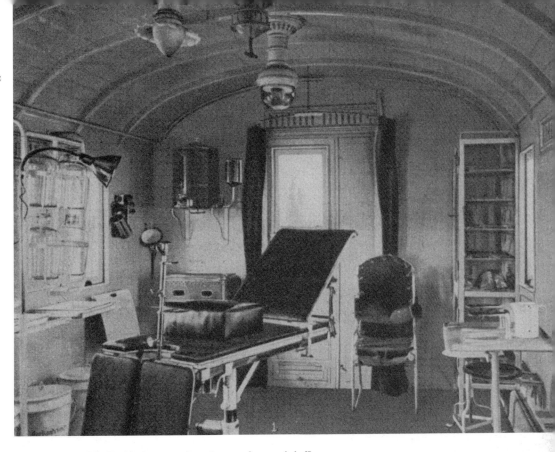

Archduke Charles Stephan of Austrian and the President of the Austro-Hungarian Society of Orthopaedists leaves the Reichstag after attending a meeting of the German Orthopaedic Society.

Lounging room for wounded officers.

Above: A war laundry. Such operations were designed to wash large quantities of clothing en masse.

Left: Born, age 17, a competitor in the Crown Prince Endurance Test, crosses the finish line. He is not only the winner, but the first of approximately 600 competitors.

Opposite: A German marching band.

Munitions store.

A storeroom for rifle
cartridge shell caps.

Members of the Ruedesheimer vineyard harvest grapes.

German labourers constructing a railway tunnel pose for the camera.

Chronology of Events

1 January – Russian offensive on the Strypa and the Styr in Galicia.

6 January – First attempt to relieve Kut (Battle of Sheikh Sa'ad) fails. Although the Turks are forced to retire, heavy rains halt the British advance.

8 January – Evacuation of the Dardanelles Peninsula completed. Despite gloomy predictions, there are few casualties.

10 January – Start of the Russian winter offensive in the Caucasus. Turkish Third Army driven back on Erzurum, with heavy losses.

13 January – Kermanshah, west Persia, occupied by Ottoman forces.

14 January – The Battle of Wadi. British forces attempt to relieve the garrison of Kut-al-Amara. Approximately 1,600 servicemen are killed, wounded and or captured.

15 January – British steamship SS *Appam* captured by German merchant raider SMS *Möwe*.

20 January – Negotiations between Austria-Hungary and Montenegro are suspended.

21 January – First British attack on Hanna, Mesopotamia. Anglo-Indian forces advance towards the garrison of Kut-al-Amara. Encountering well-prepared Ottoman positions, they retire.

23 January – Austro-Hungarian soldiers occupy the city of Scutari, Albania. The largest city in the north, it was at centre of the zone of the occupation until the end of the war.

25 January – Austrian forces capture the seaport of San Giovanni de Medua, while a detachment of Bulgarian infantry seizes Dibra, southern Albania.

31 January – German airship *L-19* (*LZ-54*) founders in the North Sea, following raids on Birmingham and Burton-upon-Trent. In total, 61 people are killed and 101 injured.

8 February – French cruiser *Admiral Charner* sunk off the Syrian coast by SMS *U-21*, a U-19-class submarine.

9 February – German steamboat *Hedwig von Wissman* sunk by HMS *Mimi* and *Fifi* on Lake Tanganyika, effectively ending German ascendancy in East Africa.

12 February – Following a preliminary bombardment, Russian forces seized Fort Kara-Gobek, Erzurum.

17 February – Carl Zimmermann, the German commander of Kamerun, orders all remaining units to escape to the neutral Spanish colony of Rio Muni.

18 February – German forces stationed at Mora, Kamerun, surrender.

21 February – Battle of Verdun begins. German Fifth Army harries French forces defending the fortified city of Verdun-sur-Meuse. *LZ-77* brought down by French gunfire at Revigny.

23 February – Portuguese naval detachment seizes German and Austrian steamers at anchor on the River Tagus.

24 February – German soldiers capture Fort Douaumont, the largest and highest redoubt of the two concentric rings protecting the city of Verdun.

26 February – Action of Agagiya, Western Egypt. Senussi forces (supported by the Ottoman Army), suffer heavy casualties at the hands of a column of the Western Frontier Force (WFF), east of Sidi Barrani.

27 February – Durazzo captured by Austro-Hungarian troops.

29 February – German raider SMS *Greif* engages the British auxiliary cruiser HMS *Alcantara* and three armed merchant cruisers in the North Sea. Both *Alcantara* and *Greif* are sunk.

1 March – German extended submarine campaign begins. Such action was responsible, more than any other, for bringing the United States into the war.

2 March – Russian soldiers capture the town of Bitlis, southwest Turkey.

5 March – Advance on Kilimanjaro, Tanzania, begins. South African forces, under the command of Field Marshal Jan Smuts, approach from two directions.

8 March – British forces, under the command of Lieutenant General Fenton Aylmer, attempt to rescue the beleaguered garrison at Kut once again. Despite being outnumbered 2:1, Ottoman forces succeed in holding their positions.

9 March – Germany declares war on Portugal, followed by Portugal's reciprocal declaration. Under pressure from the French, the Italians launch an offensive on the Isonzo River (the Fifth Battle of Isonzo).

14 March – German Minister of Marine, Admiral von Tirpitz resigns.

15 March – Austro-Hungary severs diplomatic relations with Portugal. War is declared later that day.

17 March – Following a week of heavy fighting, at the cost of 4,000 lives on both sides, the Fifth Battle of the Isonzo is concluded.

18 March – Lake Naroch Offensive begins. The Russian Second Army attacks the German line. However, owing to well-fortified defences, Russian troops fail to neutralise the defenders.

21 March – German forces, in danger of being encircled and overrun, retire from positions at the base of Mount Kilimanjaro.

24 March – Cross-English Channel passenger ferry *Sussex* torpedoed by SMS *UB-29*. The attack sparked outraged in the United States, despite the fact that no US citizens were killed.

31 March – German airship *L-15* brought down by gunfire, 15 miles north of Margate. One crewmember drowns and the rest surrender having scuttled the airship.

4 April – After several months at sea and numerous ships sunk, the German raider SMS *Möwe* returns home to Bremen and a hero's welcome.

5 April – British forces capture Ottoman trenches at Falahiya, Mesopotamia. Resistance is negligible and the objective is taken with ease.

11 April – Portuguese forces recapture Kionga, German East Africa, and present-day Mozambique.

14 April – Aircraft of the RNAS (Royal Naval Air Service) carry out bombing raids on Constantinople and Adrianople, Turkey.

17 April – Italian government issues decree prohibiting trade with Germany.

19 April – Kondoa Irangi in German East Africa is seized by British troops.

20 April – SS *Libau*, a German merchant steam ship masquerading as the transport vessel *Aud*, is scuttled by her crew. Laden with an estimated 20,000 rifles, 1,000,000 rounds of ammunition and 10 machine guns, she was destined for Ireland in preparation for the Easter Rising.

22 April – British 17th Division attacks Ottoman positions at Sannaiyat. Though initially successful, they are ultimately forced to retire in the face of heavy opposition.

24 April – Rebellion breaks out in Ireland. Irish Volunteers, led by Patrick Pearse, a schoolmaster and Irish language activist, seize key locations in Dublin and proclaim an Irish Republic.

25 April – Lowestoft and Yarmouth raided by a German battle cruiser squadron.

26 April – French and Russian governments conclude Sykes-Picot agreement partitioning Asia Minor.

27 April – As a result of the armed insurrection, martial law is proclaimed across the county of Dublin. HMS *Russell*, a British Duncan-class pre-dreadnought battleship, is sunk off the coast of Malta by a German sea mine.

29 April – Anglo-Indian garrison surrenders at Kut-al-Amara. Losses on both sides are high, anywhere between 10–20,000 casualties. A further 7,000 British soldiers die while in captivity.

30 April – After several weeks of fighting, the Battle of Lake Naroch ends in failure. What ground the Russians initially seize is recaptured by German forces.

1 May – Irish Rebellion collapses. Patrick Pearse and the members of the Irish Volunteers agree to an unconditional surrender.

3 May – German airship *L-20* wrecked at Stavanger (Norway), returning from a raid on Scotland.

4 May – *L-7* brought down by the British light-cruisers HMS *Phaeton* and *Galatea* off the coast of Slesvig.

5 May – *LZ-85* shot down by HMS *Agamemnon* at Salonika. Serbian forces capture twelve members of the crew, including the commanding officer.

7 May – Ottoman forces retire in the face of the Russian advance at Qasr-e-Shirin, northwest Iran.

9 May – British and French governments conclude Sykes-Picot agreement.

14 May – Opening bombardment by 400 field guns signals the start of the Austro-Hungarian offensive (the Battle of Asiago) in Trentino.

21 May – German troops storm the lowlands surrounding Vimy Ridge following a preliminary bombardment and the detonation of a mine beneath the British front line.

25 May – British forces advance across the frontier into German East Africa, from the direction of Northern Rhodesia and Nyasaland.

27 May – German units stationed at Neu Langenburg, German East Africa, surrender to the British.

31 May – British Grand Fleet ambushes German High Seas Fleet off the coast of Norway. Turkish forces retake Mamakhatun.

1 June – Battle of Jutland ends. Combined German and British casualties are approximately 10,000, along with 26 ships sunk.

2 June – Trentino Offensive stabilises. Battle of Mount Sorrell begins. German forces launch an offensive against the Allied front line.

3 June – German soldiers storm Fort Vaux, Verdun, after a 2,000-shells-an-hour barrage.

4 June – In an effort to relieve pressure on the Western Front, the Russian Army launches the Brusilov Offensive.

5 June – HMS *Hampshire* sunk by a mine off the Scottish coast with the loss of 737 lives. Notable fatalities include Field Marshal Earl Kitchener and his staff.

8 June – Bismarckburg, German East Africa, seized by the British.

10 June – Sharif of Mecca incites revolt in the Muslim holy city of Mecca. The insurrection is directed against the Ottoman Caliphate. 3,500 Arabs supported by British warships and seaplanes attack the port city of Jeddah. German forces, commanded by General Paul von Lettow-Vorbeck, are repulsed at Kondoa Irangi, German East Africa.

13 June – After eleven days of fighting, German troops withdraw in the face of repeat counterattacks from Mount Sorrell.

16 June – The Ottoman garrison stationed at Jeddah surrenders to Allied forces. Italian counter-offensive in the Trentino begins.

19 June – British Imperial forces capture Handeni, German East Africa.

20 June – Qasr-e-Shirin, West Persia, is retaken by Ottoman troops.

23 June – Repeated attacks against Fort Thiaumont finally prove successful and German forces capture a section of the redoubt.

24 June – Austrians are driven out of Bukovina.

30 June – French infantry recapture Fort Thiaumont.

1 July – British and French forces attack the German line between Gommecourt and Hattencourt on the Somme. British casualties are approximately 60,000. German casualties are between 10–12,000.

2 July – The Russian Western Front Army launches an attack in the region of Baranovichi. It coincides with a similar offensive to the southwest.

7 July – British forces occupy Tanga, German East Africa.

10 July – Russian hospital ship *Vpered* torpedoed by SM *U-38* in the Black Sea between Rizeh and Batum and sinks shortly thereafter.

11 July – German submarine shells Seaham, a coal-exporting town on the coast of Durham.

14 July – British Fourth Army launches a dawn raid against the German position at Bazentin on the Somme. Cavalry are employed to limited effect. Commonwealth forces seize Mwanza, German East Africa. 1st South African Brigade advances toward the southwest corner of Delville Wood (Bois d'Elville) on the Somme.

17 July – Battle of Bazentin Ridge ends. The Allied success was as a result of the weight and accuracy of the preliminary bombardment.

19 July – Soldiers of the Australian Imperial Force (AIF) attack the German front line between the Fauquissart-Trivelet road and Cordonnerie Farm.

23 July – Hoping to menace the German bastion of Thiepval, Australian troops launch a series of attacks in and around the village of Pozières, Somme.

25 July – Erzinjan, Armenia, captured by Russian forces. This was the furthest point west attained by Russian soldiers.

31 July – German forces cede control of Kilimatinde, in German East Africa.

3 August – Ujiji, Lake Tanganyika, German East Africa, occupied by Belgian forces.

4 August – German-Ottoman forces launch an attack on the Suez Canal. It is the last ground attack in the area and marks the end of the defence of the watercourse.

6 August – Sixth Battle of the Isonzo, also known as the Battle of Gorizia begins. The offensive was concentrated to the west of the Isonzo river and the westernmost edge of the Karst Plateau.

8 August – Portuguese government extends military co-operation to Europe.

10 August – Hamadan, Western Persia, seized by the Ottoman army.

15 August – Bagamoyo, German East Africa, taken by British troops. Mush and Bitlis, Armenia, reoccupied by Turkish troops.

17 August – Military convention signed between the Triple Entente and Rumania. In the face of overwhelming odds, Austro-Hungarian forces retire to Slovene territory, yielding control of Gorizia.

19 August – British light-cruiser HMS *Falmouth* sunk by SM *U-66* off Flamborough Head, Yorkshire.

24 August – Ottoman forces withdraw from the cities of Mush and Bitlis.

27 August – Rumania government orders full mobilisation and declares war on Austria-Hungary.

28 August – Rumanian troops cross the Hungarian frontier, invading Transylvania. German declares war on Rumania.

1 September – Bulgaria declares war on Rumania.

2 September – German and Bulgarian forces, under the command of *Generalfeldmarschall* von Mackensen, invade Dobrudja. Fourteen German airships raid London and other parts of Britain.

3 September – British Fourth Army attacks the village of Guillemont on the Somme, in order to extend the Allied right flank. Battle of Delville Wood ends. Though costly, the attack succeeds in its objective and South African forces capture the wood. Commonwealth and Allied soldiers seize the plateau north and east of the village of Pozières.

4 September – The colonial capital of German East Africa, Dar-es-Salaam, falls to Commonwealth troops.

6 September – Battle of Guillemont ends. Despite heavy casualties, British forces are ultimately successful. Tutrakan (Dobrudja) annexed by Bulgarian forces.

8 September – Elements of the Rumanian army occupy Orsova, Hungary. Fighting erupts between the Belgian *Force Publique* and remnants of the German colonial army, northwest of the town of Tabora, German East Africa.

9 September – The 16th (Irish) Division captures the German-held village of Ginchy during the Battle of Ginchy.

10 September – Combined Bulgarian-German forces advance into Dobrudja, annexing Silistra (a port city in north-eastern Bulgaria).

14 September – Rather than repeat the broad-based diversionary attacks of earlier offensives, Italian forces conduct a series of tightly focused initiatives. Each is directed at a single target along the Isonzo front and are all part of the Seventh Battle of the Isonzo.

15 September – Battle of Flers-Courcelette, Somme, begins. For the first time in history, tanks are employed on the battlefield.

18 September – Seventh Battle of the Isonzo ends. Tightly focused initiatives combined with sustained bombardment effectively reduce the Austro-Hungarian will to fight, and Italian troops seize Nova Vas.

19 September – After eleven days of fighting the Belgian *Force Publique* captures Tabora, the largest town in German East Africa.

22 September – Turkish garrison of Taif surrenders to Arab forces. Battle of Flers-Courcelette ends with the capture of Courcelette, Martinpuich and Flers by Allied forces.

23 September – German Zeppelins bomb London and the east coast of England, killing 170 people. *L-32* and *L-33* are destroyed.

24 September – Two pilots of the French air force, attack the Krupp munitions works at Essen. Twelve bombs are dropped but little damage is caused.

25 September – British Fourth and the French Sixth armies attack the German lines on the Somme, between Gueudecourt in the north and Combles in the south.

26 September – Battle of Thiepval Ridge. Allied forces launch an offensive from Courcelette in the east to Thiepval and the Schwaben Redoubt in the west.

28 September – German First Army withdraws from Combles, Morval, Lesboeufs and Gueudecourt, following sustained Allied attacks. Battle of Thiepval Ridge ends, the allies having failed to secure their final objectives.

1 October – French and Commonwealth forces attack the German line at Le Transloy on the Somme. Battle of the Ancre Heights begins. British Reserve Army (later renamed, Fifth Army) advances from Courcelette, near the Albert-Bapaume road, and west to Thiepval.

7 October – After heavy fighting, Austro-German forces retake Brasov, Transylvania.

SM *U-53* captures five ships outside Newport, Rhode Island. After careful inspection, each craft is destroyed.

9 October – Hoping to extend the bridgehead established at the Seventh Battle of the Isonzo, Italian troops launch a series of probing attacks to the left of Gorizia.

12 October – After several days of bitter and intense fighting, the offensive launched at Gorizia is postponed. Both nations retire in order to resupply and reorganise.

14 October – German forces cross the Rumanian frontier at Transylvania.

17 October – Affair in the Dakhla Oasis, West Egypt, begins.

18 October – Battle of Le Transloy ends.

21 October – Friedrich Adler, son of the Social Democratic party chairman Victor Adler, shoots Count Karl von Stürgkh, the Austrian Premier.

22 October – The Central Powers seize Constanza, Rumania's primary Black Sea port.

24 October – The French Second Army recaptures Fort Douaumont after months of heavy fighting. The fort had been subjected to artillery fire for two days prior to the attack and the defenders were in the process of evacuating.

25 October – Cernavoda captured by Bulgarian soldiers.

26 October – German torpedo boats of the III and IX Flanders Flotilla launch a raid into the Dover Strait.

29 October – Sharif of Mecca is proclaimed 'King of the Arabs'.

31 October – Ninth Battle of the Isonzo begins. Italian forces, in an attempt to extend their bridgehead to the left of the town of Gorizia, launch a major offensive.

1 November – German infantry abandons Fort Vaux, Verdun, after months of shelling. The fort is retaken that day by French forces.

4 November – After heavy fighting the Ninth Battle of the Isonzo ends. Casualties on both sides are high.

5 November – Germany and Austria proclaim an Independent State of Poland.

11 November – Battle of the Ancre Heights, Somme, ends. After a series of large-scale attacks, Anglo-French soldiers seized 1,000 yards of ground.

13 November – Anglo-French forces launch a series of small offensives on the Somme.

15 November – 5,000 Mohmands, a Pashtun tribe, are routed at the Third Affair of Hafiz Kor, North-West Frontier of India.

18 November – Despite heavy German opposition, Entente forces capture Beaumont Hamel, St Pierre Divion and Beaucourt. Their seizure signals the end of the Battle of the Somme.

21 November – Craiova, Rumania, annexed by German troops.

22 November – Austro-German forces seize Orsova, Hungary. German commerce raider *Seeadler* leaves Germany.

23 November – Provisional Greek government declares war on Bulgaria and Germany.

26 November – Following the success of the first raid on Lowestoft, the German High Seas Fleet launches a second raid on the English port town.

27 November – *L-34* destroyed by Second Lieutenant Ian Pyott off the east coast of England, following a raid on Hartlepool.

28 November – Lone German aircraft bombs London. This was first daylight raid by an aeroplane over England.

1 December – Rumanian Army launches an offensive along the Argeș River, the last natural barrier before the capital, Bucharest.

3 December – SM *U-38*, under the command of Max Valentiner, torpedoes SS *Kanguroo*, *Surprise* and CS *Dacia* in Funchal harbour, Madeira.

5 December – Despite early successes, the Rumanian army fails to take Bucharest and is routed by German forces.

11 December – General Joffre, Commander-in-Chief of the French forces and advisor to the Serbian army, calls off the offensives at the Cerna River and Monastir.

18 December – After 303 days of fighting, the German offensive at Verdun is suspended. A combined estimate of 1,250,000 casualties is sustained.

21 December – El Arish, Sinai, occupied by British forces.

23 December – Egyptian Expeditionary Force (EEF) launches an attack to the south and east of Bir Lahfan, Sinai.

30 December – Entente government rejects German peace proposal.

31 December – Felix Yusupov murders Grigori Rasputin, Russian mystic and friend of Tsar Nicholas II.

Bibliography

Archival Sources

Daily Mirror, 'The Battle of Jutland', 3 June 1916, British Library, London (BL).

The Times, 5 February 1916, British Library, London (BL).

The Times, 'Bishop of London and the Skipper', 7 February 1916, British Library, London (BL).

Wallace, A., Letter to fiancée Ethel, 14 November 1916, National Army Museum, London (NAM), 1991-03-43-65.

Secondary Sources

Allen, K., 'Sharing Scarcity: Bread Rationing and the First World War in Berlin, 1914-1923', *Journal of Social History*, 32 (2) 1998.

Allen, W.E.D. and Muratoff, P., *Caucasian Battlefields, A History of Wars on the Turco-Caucasian Border, 1828-1921* (Cambridge: Cambridge University Press, 2011).

Anderson, R., *The Forgotten Front: The East African Campaign; 1914-1918* (Cheltenham: Tempus Publishing Ltd, 2004).

Atrash, N., 'Mapping Palestine: The Bavarian Air Force WWI Aerial Photography', *Jerusalem Quarterly*, 56 (1) 2014.

Baker, L. and Cooling, B.F., 'Developments and Lessons Before World War II', in B. F. Cooling (eds.), *Case Studies in the Achievement of Air Superiority* (Washington: Air Force History and Museums Program, 1994).

Bell, C.M., *Churchill and the Dardanelles* (Oxford: Oxford University Press, 2017).

Bilton, D., *The Central Powers on the Russian Front: Rare Photographs from Wartime Archives* (Barnsley: Pen & Sword Military, 2014).

Black, J., *Air Power: A Global History* (Maryland: The Rowman & Littlefield Publishing Group, Inc, 2016).

Boff, J., *Winning and Losing on the Western Front: The British Third Army and the Defeat of Germany in 1918* (Cambridge: Cambridge University Press, 2012).

Brennan, J.R. and Burton, A., 'The Emerging Metropolis: A history of Dar es Salaam, circa 1862–2000', in J. R. Brennan, A. Burton and Y. Q. Lawi (eds.), *Dar es Salaam. Histories from an Emerging African Metropolis* (Oxford: African Books Collective, 2007).

Brooks, J., *The Battle of Jutland* (Cambridge: Cambridge University Press, 2016).

Bruce, R.B., 'To the Last Limits of Their Strength: The French Army and the Logistics of Attrition at the Battle of Verdun, 21 February–18 December 1916', *Army History*, 45 (1) 1998.

Burg, D. F. and Purcell, L. E., *Almanac of World War I* (Lexington: The University Press of Kentucky, 1998).

Campbell, J., *Jutland: An Analysis of the Fighting* (Guildford: Lyons Press, 1998).

Canwell, D. and Sutherland, J., *The Battle of Jutland* (Barnsley: Pen & Sword Maritime, 2007).

Catherwood, C., *The Battles of World War I* (London: Allison & Busby, 2014).

Cimpri, Z. and Macdonald, J., *Caporetto and the Isonzo Campaign: The Italian Front 1915-1918* (Barnsley: Pen & Sword Military, 2011).

Clark, A., *The Donkeys* (London: Pimlico, 2011).

Clodfelter, M., *Warfare and Armed Conflicts: A Statistical Encyclopedia of Casualty and Other Figures, 1492–2015* (Jefferson: McFarland & Company, Inc., Publishers, 2017).

Cockfield, J.H., *Russia's Iron General: The Life of Aleksei A. Brusilov, 1853–1926* (London: Lexington Books, 2019).

Corum, J.S. and Muller, R.R., 'Instructions on the Mission and Utilization of Flying Units within the Army', In J. S. Corum and R. R. Muller (eds.), *The Luftwaffe's Way of War. German Air Doctrine, 1911–1945* (Baltimore, MD: Nautical & *Aviation* Publishing, 1998).

David, S., *1916: Verdun to the Somme: Key Dates and Events from the Third Year of the First World War* (London: Hodder & Stoughton, 2013).

Deverell, C., 'Haig versus Rawlinson-Manoeuvre versus Attrition: The British Army on the Somme, 1916', *Defence Studies*, 5 (1) 2005.

Erickson, E.J., *Gallipoli & the Middle East 1914–1918: From the Dardanelles to Mesopotamia* (London: Amber Books Ltd, 2011).

Erickson, E., *Ordered to Die: A History of the Ottoman Army in the First World War* (London: Greenwood Press, 2001).

Fallada, H., *Little Man, What Now?* (London: Melville House Publishing, 2009).

Faulks, S., *Birdsong* (New York: Vintage, 1994).

Ferguson, N., *The Pity of War* (London: Penguin Books, 1999).

Foley, R., 'Learning War's Lessons: The German Army and the Battle of the Somme 1916', *Journal of Military History*, 75 (2) 2011.

Foley, R., *German Strategy and the Path to Verdun* (Cambridge: Cambridge University Press, 2004).

Franks, N.L R., Bailey, F. W. and Guest, R., *Above the Lines: The Aces and Fighter Units of the German Air Service, Naval Air Service and Flanders Marine Corps 1914–1918* (London: Grub Street, 1993).

Fritzsche, P., *Germans into Nazis* (London: Harvard University Press, 2000).

Garipey, P., *Gardens of Hell: Battles of the Gallipoli Campaign* (Lincoln: Potomac Books, 2014).

Geinitz, C., 'Strategic Bombing of German Cities', in R. Chickering and S. Förster (eds.), *Great War, Total War: Combat and Mobilization on the Western Front, 1914-1918* (Cambridge: Cambridge University Press, 2000).

Gooch, J., *The Italian Army and the First World War* (Cambridge: Cambridge University Press, 2014).

Gray, E., *Captains of War: They Fought Beneath the Sea* (London: Leo Cooper Ltd, 1988).

Gröner, E., Jung, D. and Maass, M., *U-boats and Mine Warfare Vessels. German Warships 1815–1945* (London: Conway Maritime Press, 1991).

Harris, J.P., *Douglas Haig and the First World War* (Cambridge: Cambridge University Press, 2008).

Head, R.G., *Oswald Boelcke: Germany's First Fighter Ace and Father of Air Combat* (London: Grub Street, 2016).

Heer, H. and Naumann, K., *War of Extermination: The German Military in World War II, 1941–44* (New York: Berghahn Books, 2000).

Herwig, H.H., *The First World War: Germany and Austro-Hungary 1914–1918* (London: Bloomsbury Academic, 2014).

Hillmann, J., 'Remembering the Battle of Jutland in Germany', In M. Epkenhans, J. Hillmann and F. Nägler (eds.), *Jutland: World War I's Greatest Naval Battle* (Lexington: The University Press of Kentucky, 2015).

Hinterhoff, E., *Persia: The Stepping Stone to India. Marshall Cavendish Illustrated Encyclopedia of World War I* (New York: Marshall Cavendish Corporation, 1984).

Hitler, A., *Hitler's Secret Conversations* (New York: Farar, Straus and Young, 1953).

Horne, J., 'War, Law, and the *Levée en masse* from 1870 to 1945', in Moran, D. and Waldron, A. (eds.), *The People in Arms: Military Myth and National Mobilization Since the French Revolution* (Cambridge: Cambridge University Press, 2006).

Jackson, A., 'Germany, The Home Front (2): Blockade, Government and Revolution', In H. Cecil and P. Liddle (eds.), *Facing Armageddon: The First World War Experience* (London: Leo Cooper, 1996).

Jordan, D. and Neiberg, M.S., *The Eastern Front 1914–1920: From Tannenberg to the Russo-Polish War* (London: Amber Books Ltd, 2011).

Kinross, P., *Atatürk: The Rebirth of a Nation* (London: Weidenfeld and Nicolson, 2012).

Knight, P., *The British Army in Mesopotamia, 1914-1918* (London: McFarland & Company, Inc., Publishers, 2013).

Knox, A.W.F., *With the Russian Army, 1914–1917, Vol. II* (London: Hutchinson & Co, 1921).

Lettow-Vorbeck, P.E., *My Reminiscences of East Africa: The East Africa Campaign of the First World War by the Most Notable German Commander* (Uckfield: Naval and Military Press, 2009).

Liman von Sanders, O., *Five Years in Turkey* (Uckfield: The Naval and Military Press Ltd, 2012).

Lincoln, W.B., *Passage through Armageddon. The Russians in War and Revolution, 1914-1918* (New York: Simon & Schuster, 1986).

Loewenberg, P.P., 'Germany, The Home Front (I): The Physical and Psychological Consequences of Home Front Hardship', in H. Cecil and P. Liddle (eds.), *Facing Armageddon: The First World War Experience* (London: Leo Cooper, 1996).

de Matos Machado, R. and Hupy, J.P., 'The Conflict Landscape of Verdun, France: Conserving Cultural and Natural Heritage After WWI', In Todd R. Lookingbill, Peter D. Smallwood (eds.), *Collateral Values: The Natural Capital Created by Landscapes of War* (New York: Springer, 2019).

McNabb, J.B., 'Egypt', In S. Tucker (ed.), *World War I: A Student Encyclopedia. Vol. I: A–D* (Oxford: ABC-CLIO, 2006).

Middlebrook, M., *The First Day on the Somme* (London: Allen Lane, 1971).

Miller, C., *Battle for the Bundu: The First World War in East Africa* (New York: Macmillan, 1974).

Miller, R., *Trenchard: Father of the Royal Air Force* (London: Weidenfeld and Nicolson, 2017).

Morrow, Jr., J.H., *The Great War: An Imperial History* (London: Routledge, 2004).

Mortlok, M.J., *The Egyptian Expeditionary Force in World War I: A History of the British-Led Campaigns in Egypt, Palestine and Syria* (Jefferson: McFarland & Company, Inc., Publishers, 2011).

Moyse-Bartlett, H., *The King's African Rifles: A Study in the Military History of East and Central Africa, 1890–1945* (Uckfield: Naval and Military Press Ltd, 2012).

Murphy, J.D., *Military Aircraft, Origins to 1918: An Illustrated History of Their Impact* (Oxford: ABC-CLIO, 2005).

Neiberg, M.S., and Jordan, D., *The Eastern Front 1914–1920: The History of World War I: From Tannenberg to Russo-Polish War* (London: Amber Books Ltd, 2012).

Neiberg, M.S., *Fighting the Great War: A Global History* (Harvard: Harvard University Press, 2009).

Nicolle, D., *The Ottoman Army 1914-1918* (Oxford: Osprey, 1994).

Osborne, R., *The Battle of Jutland: History's Greatest Sea Battle Told Through Newspaper Reports, Official Documents and the Accounts of Those Who Were There* (Barnsley: Pen & Sword Books Ltd, 2016).

Philpott, W., *Attrition: Fighting the First World War* (London: Little, Brown, 2014).

Philpott, W., *Bloody Victory: The Sacrifice on the Somme and the Making of the Twentieth Century* (London: Little, Brown, 2009).

Philpott, W., 'The Anglo-French Victory on the Somme', *Diplomacy & Statecraft*, 17 (4) 2006.

Podorozhniy, N.E., *The Naroch Offensive in March 1916 on the Russian Front of the World War* (Moscow: Voenizdat, 1938).

Prior, P. and T. Wilson, T., *The Somme* (Yale: Yale University Press, 2016).

Pudasaini, S.P. and Hutter, K., *Avalanche Dynamics: Dynamics of Rapid Flows of Dense Granular Avalanches* (New York: Springer-Verlag Berlin Heidelberg, 2007).

Rahn, W., 'The Battle of Jutland from the German perspective', M. Epkenhans, J. Hillmann, F. Nägler (eds.), *Jutland: World War I's Greatest Naval Battle* (Lexington: The University Press of Kentucky, 2015).

Raleigh, W.A., *The War in the Air: Being the Story of the Part Played in the Great War by the Royal Air Force, Volume 6* (Oxford: Clarendon Press, 1937).

Rasor, E., *The Battle of Jutland. A Bibliography* (Westport, CT: Greenwood Press, 1992).

Rochat, G., 'The Italian Front, 1915–18', in J. Horne (ed.), *A Companion to World War I* (Chichester: John Wiley & Sons Ltd, 2012).

Schinder, J.R., *Isonzo: The Forgotten Sacrifice of the Great War* (London: Praeger Publishers, 2001).

Schwabe, K. and Reichardt, R. (eds.), *Gerhard Ritter. Ein politischer Historiker in seinen Briefen* (Boppard: H. Boldt, 1984).

Seth, R., *Caporetto: The Scapegoat Battle* (London: Macdonald, 1965).

Sheffield, G., *The Somme* (London: Cassell, 2003).

Smith, R., *Jamaican Volunteers in the First World War: Race, Masculinity and the development of national consciousness* (Manchester: Manchester University Press, 2004.

Sondhaus, L., *World War One: The Global Revolution* (Cambridge: Cambridge University Press, 2011).

Sterling, C.H., 'Fokker Aircraft (Early Years, World War I)', in W. J. Boyne (ed.), *Air Warfare: An International Encyclopedia: A–L* (Oxford: ABC-CLIO, 2002).

Stille, M., *British Battlecruiser vs German Battlecruiser: 1914–16* (Oxford: Osprey Publishing, 2013).

Stone, N., *The Eastern Front 1914–1917* (London: Penguin Books, 1998).

Storey, W.K., *The First World War: A Concise Global History* (Plymouth: Rowman & Littlefield Publishers, Inc., 2009).

Strachan, H., *The First World War in Africa* (Oxford: Oxford University Press, 2004).

Strachan, H., *The First World War: To Arms I* (Oxford: Oxford University Press, 2001).

Tarrant, V.E., *Jutland: The German Perspective: A New View of the Great Battle, 31 May 1916* (London: Arms & Armour Press, 1995).

Thompson, M., *The White War: Life and Death on the Italian Front, 1915–1919* (London: Faber and Faber Ltd, 2009).

Trumpener, U., 'Naroch, Lake, Battle of (March 1916)', in Tucker, S. (ed.), *The European Powers in the First World War: An Encyclopedia* (London: Garland Publishing, Inc., 1996).

Tucker, S.C., 'Lake Naroch, Battle of', In S. C. Tucker (ed.), *World War I: The Definitive Encyclopedia and Document Collection, V. 1: A–C* (California: ABC-CLIO, LLC, 2014).

Tunstall, G.A., 'Austria-Hungary and the Brusilov Offensive of 1916', *The Historian*, 70 (1) 2008.

Vanwyngarden, G., *Albatros Aces of World War I Part 2: Aircraft of the Aces No. 77* (Oxford: Osprey Publishing, 2007).

Vego, M.N., *Naval Strategy and Operations in Narrow Seas* (Abingdon: Frank Cass Publishers, 2003).

Walter, D., 'Erzurum Offensive (10 January–25 March 1916)', in S. Tucker (ed.), *World War I: A Student Encyclopedia. Vol. I: A–D* (Oxford: ABC-CLIO, 2006).

Watson, A., *Ring of Steel: Germany and Austria-Hungary at War, 1914-1918* (London: Penguin Books, 2015).

Watts, T.J., 'Mesopotamian Theatre', In S. Tucker (ed.), *World War I: A Student Encyclopedia. Vol. I: A–D* (Oxford: ABC-CLIO, 2006).

Williams, A.G., and Gustin, E., *Flying Guns of World War I: Development of Aircraft Guns, Ammunition and Installations 1914–32* (Crawley: Airlife, 2004).

Internet Sources

Davis, B., 'Food and Nutrition (Germany)', *International Encyclopedia for First World War Studies* [Online], 2014. URL: https://encyclopedia.1914-1918-online.net/article/food_and_nutrition_germany

Dowling, T.C., 'Eastern Front', *International Encyclopedia of First World War Studies* [Online], 2014. URL: https://encyclopedia.1914-1918-online.net/article/eastern_front

Krause, J., 'Western Front', *International Encyclopedia of the First World War* [Online], 2014. URL: https://encyclopedia.1914-1918-online.net/article/western_front

Mahoney, R. and Pugh, J., 'Air Warfare', *International Encyclopedia of the First World War* [Online], 2014. URL: https://encyclopedia.1914-1918-online.net/article/air_warfare

Paice, E., 'The First World War in East Africa', *The British Library World War One* [Online], 2019. URL: https://www.bl.uk/world-war-one/articles/the-first-world-war-in-east-africa

Philpott, W., 'Somme, Battles of', *International Encyclopedia of the First World War*, [Online], 2014. URL: https://encyclopedia.1914-1918-online.net/pdf/1914-1918-Online-somme_battles_of-2014-11-01.pdf

Philpott, W., 'Warfare 1914–1918', *International Encyclopedia of the First World War* [Online], 2014. URL: https://encyclopedia.1914-1918-online.net/article/warfare_1914-1918

Wells, M., 'Aircraft, Fighter and Pursuit', *International Encyclopedia of First World War Studies* [Online], 2016. URL: https://encyclopedia.1914-1918-online.net/article/aircraft_fighter_and_pursuit

Yanıkdağ, Y., 'Ottoman Empire/Middle East', *International Encyclopedia of First World War [Online], 2014. URL:* https://encyclopedia.1914-1918-online.net/article/ottoman_empiremiddle_east

Endnotes

Introduction

1. Boff, J., *Winning and Losing on the Western Front: The British Third Army and the Defeat of Germany in 1918* (Cambridge: Cambridge University Press, 2012), pp.74–122.

2. Herwig, H.H., *The First World War: Germany and Austro-Hungary 1914–1918* (London: Bloomsbury Academic, 2014), p.181

3. Bruce, R.B., 'To the Last Limits of Their Strength: The French Army and the Logistics of Attrition at the Battle of Verdun, 21 February–18 December 1916', *Army History*, 45 (1) 1998, p.9.

4. Philpott, W., 'Somme, Battles of', *International Encyclopaedia of the First World War*, [Online], 2014. URL: https://encyclopedia.1914-1918-online.net/pdf/1914-1918-Online-somme_battles_of-2014-11-01.pdf

5. Ibid.

6. Foley, R., 'Learning War's Lessons: The German Army and the Battle of the Somme 1916', *Journal of Military History*, 75 (2) 2011, p.500.

7. Mahoney, R. and Pugh, J., 'Air Warfare', *International Encyclopedia of First World War* [Online], 2018. URL: https://encyclopedia.1914-1918-online.net/article/air_warfare

8. Franks, N.L.R., Bailey, F.W. and Guest, R., *Above the Lines: The Aces and Fighter Units of the German Air Service, Naval Air Service and Flanders Marine Corps 1914–1918* (London: Grub Street, 1993), pp.4, 29–56.

9. Neiberg, M.S., and Jordan, D., *The Eastern Front 1914–1920: The History of World War I: From Tannenberg to Russo-Polish War* (London: Amber Books Ltd, 2012), p.86.

10. S.C. Tucker, 'Lake Naroch, Battle of', in S. C. Tucker (ed.), *World War I: The Definitive Encyclopedia and Document Collection, V. 1: A–C* (California: ABC-CLIO, LLC, 2014), p.51.

11. Bilton, D., *The Central Powers on the Russian Front: Rare Photographs from Wartime Archives* (Barnsley: Pen & Sword Military, 2014), p.71.

12. Clodfelter, M., *Warfare and Armed Conflicts: A Statistical Encyclopedia of Casualty and Other Figures, 1492–2015* (Jefferson: McFarland & Company, Inc., Publishers, 2017), p.411.

13. E.J. Erickson, *Ordered to Die: A History of the Ottoman Army in the First World War* (Westport, CT: Greenwood Press, 2001), p.120.

14. Ibid., p. 149.

15. A. Watson, *Ring of Steel: Germany and Austria-Hungary at War, 1914–1918* (London: Penguin, 2015), p.282.

16. S. Cobb, *Preparing for Blockade 1885-1914: Naval Contingency for Economic Warfare* (London: Routledge, 2016); S. Dunn, *Blockade: Cruiser Warfare and the Starvation of Germany in World War One* (Barnsley: Pen & Sword Books Ltd, 2016); E.W. Osborne, *Britain's Economic Blockade of Germany, 1914-1919* (London: Frank Cass, 2004).

Chapter 1: Westfront

1. Middlebrook, M., *The First Day on the Somme* (London: Allen Lane, 1971), p.123.
2. Clark, A., *The Donkeys* (London: Pimlico, 2011); Faulks, S., *Birdsong* (New York: Vintage, 1994).
3. de Matos Machado, R. and Hupy, J.R., 'The Conflict Landscape of Verdun, France: Conserving Cultural and Natural Heritage After WWI', in T.R. Lookingbill, P.D. Smallwood (eds.), *Collateral Values: The Natural Capital Created by Landscapes of War* (New York: Springer, 2019), p.117.
4. Philpott, W., *Attrition: Fighting the First World War* (London: Little, Brown, 2014).
5. Herwig, *The First World War: Germany and Austro-Hungary 1914–1918*, p.181.
6. Burg, D.F. and Purcell, L.E., *Almanac of World War I* (Lexington: The University Press of Kentucky, 1998), p.112.
7. Philpott, *Attrition: Fighting the First World War*, p.225.
8. Ibid., p.226.
9. Foley, R., *German Strategy and the Path to Verdun* (Cambridge: Cambridge University Press, 2004), p.256.
10. Heer, H. and Naumann, K., *War of Extermination: The German Military in World War II, 1941–44* (New York: Berghahn Books, 2000), p. 26.
11. Morrow, Jr., J.H., *The Great War: An Imperial History* (London: Routledge, 2004), p.129.
12. Philpott, W., *Bloody Victory: The Sacrifice on the Somme and the Making of the Twentieth Century* (London: Little, Brown, 2009), pp.81, 86.
13. Smith, R., *Jamaican Volunteers in the First World War: Race, Masculinity and the development of national consciousness* (Manchester: Manchester University Press, 2004), p.13.
14. Middlebrook, *The First Day on the Somme*, p.123.
15. Ibid., p.58.
16. Ibid., pp.57–65.
17. Harris, J.P., *Douglas Haig and the First World War* (Cambridge: Cambridge University Press, 2008), pp.234–237.
18. Philpott, *Blood Victory: The Sacrifice on the Somme and the Making of the Twentieth Century*, p.98.
19. Sheffield, G., *The Somme* (London: Cassell, 2003), pp.41–69.
20. Philpott, W., *Attrition: Fighting the First World War* (London: Little, Brown, 2014), p.233.

21. Schwabe, K. and Reichardt, R. (eds.), *Gerhard Ritter. Ein politischer Historiker in seinen Briefen* (Boppard: H. Boldt, 1984), pp.202–3.
22. Clark, *The Donkeys*, p.144.
23. Deverell, C., 'Haig versus Rawlinson-Manoeuvre versus Attrition: The British Army on the Somme, 1916', *Defence Studies*, 5 (1) 2005, pp.124–137; W. Philpott, 'The Anglo-French Victory on the Somme', *Diplomacy & Statecraft*, 17 (4) 2006, pp.731–751.
24. Foley, 'Learning War's Lessons: The German Army and the Battle of the Somme 1916', pp.471–504.
25. Prior, R. and Wilson, T., The Somme (Yale: Yale University Press, 2016), p.301.
26. Philpott, W., 'Warfare 1914–1918', *International Encyclopedia of the First World War* [Online], 2014. URL: https://encyclopedia.1914-1918-online.net/article/warfare_1914-1918

Chapter 2: Ostfront

1. Dowling, T.C., 'Eastern Front', *International Encyclopedia of First World War Studies* [Online], 2014. URL: https://encyclopedia.1914-1918-online.net/article/eastern_front
2. Bilton, *The Central Powers on the Russian Front: Rare Photographs from Wartime Archives*, p. 69.
3. Neiberg and Jordan, *The Eastern Front 1914–1920: From Tannenberg to the Russo-Polish War*, pp.42–44.
4. Clodfelter, *Warfare and Armed Conflicts: A Statistical Encyclopedia of Casualty and Other Figures, 1492–2015*, p.410.
5. Stone, N., *The Eastern Front 1914–1917* (London: Penguin Books, 1998), p.221, 252.
6. Neiberg, M.S., *Fighting the Great War: A Global History* (Harvard: Harvard University Press, 2009), p.178.
7. Jordan and Neiberg, *The Eastern Front 1914–1920: From Tannenberg to the Russo-Polish War*, pp.45–46.
8. Bilton, *The Central Powers on the Russian Front: Rare Photographs from Wartime Archives*, p.69.
9. Dowling, 'Eastern Front'.
10. Trumpener, U., 'Naroch, Lake, Battle of (March 1916)', in Spencer Tucker (ed.), *The European Powers in the First World War: An Encyclopedia* (London: Garland Publishing, Inc., 1996), p.501.
11. Cockfield, J.H., *Russia's Iron General: The Life of Aleksei A. Brusilov, 1853–1926* (London: Lexington Books, 2019), p.207.
12. Podorozhniy, N.E., *The Naroch Offensive in March 1916 on the Russian Front of the World War* (Moscow: Voenizdat, 1938), p. 149.
13. Ibid., pp.124–125.
14. Stone, *The Eastern Front 1914-1917*, p.231.

15. Jordan and Neiberg, *The Eastern Front 1914–1920: From Tannenberg to the Russo-Polish War*, p.47.
16. Ibid., p.51.
17. Ibid.
18. Dowling, T., *The Brusilov Offensive* (Bloomington: Indiana University Press, 2008), pp.43–44.
19. Herwig, *The First World War: Germany and Austria-Hungary 1914-1918*, p.203.
20. Cockfield, *Russia's Iron General: The Life of Aleksei A. Brusilov, 1853–1926*, p.144.
21. Herwig, *The First World War: Germany and Austria-Hungary 1914-1918*, p.203.
22. Dowling, *The Brusilov Offensive*, p.62.
23. Cockfield, *Russia's Iron General: The Life of Aleksei A. Brusilov, 1853–1926*, p.172.
24. Bilton, *The Central Powers on the Russian Front: Rare Photographs from Wartime Archives*, p.71.
25. Jordan and Neiberg, *The Eastern Front 1914–1920: From Tannenberg to the Russo-Polish War*, p.53.
26. Dowling, *The Brusilov Offensive*, p.166.
27. Clodfelter, *Warfare and Armed Conflicts: A Statistical Encyclopedia of Casualty and Other Figures, 1492–2015*, p.411.
28. Ibid., p.411.
29. Tunstall, G. A., 'Austria-Hungary and the Brusilov Offensive of 1916', *The Historian*, 70 (1) 2008, p.52.
30. Stone, *The Eastern Front 1914–1917*, p. 112.
31. Cockfield, Dowling, *The Brusilov Offensive*, p.163.
32. Dowling, 'Eastern Front'.
33. Lincoln, W.B., *Passage through Armageddon. The Russians in War and Revolution, 1914-1918* (New York: Simon & Schuster, 1986), p.260.

Chapter 3: Gebirgskrieg

1. Schinder, J.R., *Isonzo: The Forgotten Sacrifice of the Great War* (London: Praeger Publishers, 2001), p.129.
2. Philpott, 'Warfare, 1914–1918'.
3. Schinder, *Isonzo: The Forgotten Sacrifice of the Great War*, p.130.
4. Ibid., p.206.
5. Ibid., p.202.
6. For more information, see Cimpri, Z. and Macdonald, J., *Caporetto and the Isonzo Campaign: The Italian Front 1915-1918* (Barnsley: Pen & Sword Military, 2011); Schinder, *Isonzo: The Forgotten Sacrifice of the Great War*; Thompson, M., *The White War: Life and Death on the Italian Front, 1915–1919* (London: Faber and Faber Ltd, 2009).
7. Schinder, *Isonzo: The Forgotten Sacrifice of the Great War*, p.141.

8. Thompson, *The White War: Life and Death on the Italian Front, 1915–1919*, pp.157–158.
9. Ibid., p.130.
10. Seth, R., *Caporetto: The Scapegoat Battle* (London: Macdonald, 1965), p.208.
11. Gooch, J., *The Italian Army and the First World War* (Cambridge: Cambridge University Press, 2014), p.148.
12. Rochat, G., 'The Italian Front, 1915–18', in J. Horne (ed.), *A Companion to World War I* (Chichester: John Wiley & Sons Ltd, 2012), p.86.
13. Ibid., p.153.
14. Gooch, *The Italian Army and the First World War*, p.160; Rochat, 'The Italian Front, 1915–18', p.86.
15. Herwig, *The First World War: Germany and Austria-Hungary 1914-1918*, p.200.
16. Schinder, *Isonzo: The Forgotten Sacrifice of the Great War*, p.154.
17. Cimpri and Macdonald, *Caporetto and the Isonzo Campaign: The Italian Front 1915-1918*, p.84.
18. Rochat, 'The Italian Front, 1915–18', p.86.
19. Gooch, *The Italian Army and the First World War*, p.185.
20. Ibid.
21. Schinder, *Isonzo: The Forgotten Sacrifice of the Great War*, p.171.
22. Thompson, *The White War: Life and Death on the Italian Front, 1915–1919*, p.120.
23. Pudasaini, S.P. and Hutter, K., *Avalanche Dynamics: Dynamics of Rapid Flows of Dense Granular Avalanches* (New York: Springer-Verlag Berlin Heidelberg, 2007), p.75.
24. Gooch, *The Italian Army and the First World War*, p.146

Chapter 4: Türkei

1. See, Bell, C.M., *Churchill and the Dardanelles* (Oxford: Oxford University Press, 2017), pp.7–9; Garipey, P., *Gardens of Hell: Battles of the Gallipoli Campaign* (Lincoln: Potomac Books, 2014), pp.3–4.
2. *Yanıkdağ, Y., 'Ottoman Empire/Middle East', International Encyclopedia of First World War [Online], 2014.* URL: https://encyclopedia.1914-1918-online.net/article/ottoman_empiremiddle_east
3. Erickson, E., *Ordered to Die: A History of the Ottoman Army in the First World War* (London: Greenwood Press, 2001), p.119.
4. Liman von Sanders, O., *Five Years in Turkey* (Uckfield: The Naval and Military Press Ltd, 2012), p.132.
5. Horne, J., 'War, Law, and the *Levée en masse* from 1870 to 1945', in D. Moran and A. Waldron (eds.), *The People in Arms: Military Myth and National Mobilization Since the French Revolution* (Cambridge: Cambridge University Press, 2006), p.117.
6. Hitler, A., *Hitler's Secret Conversations* (New York: Farar, Straus and Young, 1953), p.25.

7. Catherwood, C., *The Battles of World War I* (London: Allison & Busby, 2014), pp. 51–52.

8. Sanders, *Five Years in Turkey*, p.132.

9. Watts, T. J., 'Mesopotamian Theatre', in S. Tucker (ed.), *World War I: A Student Encyclopedia. Vol. I: A–D* (Oxford: ABC-CLIO, 2006), p.1233.

10. McNabb, J.B., 'Egypt', in S. Tucker (ed.), *World War I: A Student Encyclopedia. Vol. I: A–D* (Oxford: ABC-CLIO, 2006), p.527.

11. Ibid., p.142.

12. Erickson, E.J., *Gallipoli & the Middle East 1914–1918: From the Dardanelles to Mesopotamia* (London: Amber Books Ltd, 2011), p.187.

13. Ibid.

14. Mortlock, M.J., *The Egyptian Expeditionary Force in World War I: A History of the British-Led Campaigns in Egypt, Palestine and Syria* (Jefferson: McFarland & Company, Inc., Publishers, 2011), p.62.

15. Sanders, *Five Years in Turkey*, p.190.

16. Hinterhoff, E., *Persia: The Stepping Stone to India. Marshall Cavendish Illustrated Encyclopedia of World War I* (New York: Marshall Cavendish Corporation, 1984), pp.499–503.

17. Walter, D., 'Erzurum Offensive (10 January–25 March 1916)', in S. Tucker (ed.), *World War I: A Student Encyclopedia. Vol. I: A–D* (Oxford: ABC-CLIO, 2006), p.646.

18. Allen, W.E.D. and Muratoff, P., *Caucasian Battlefields, A History of Wars on the Turco-Caucasian Border, 1828-1921* (Cambridge: Cambridge University Press, 2011), p.333.

19. Allen and Muratoff, *Caucasian Battlefields, A History of Wars on the Turco-Caucasian Border, 1828-1921*, p.342.

20. Ibid., p.368.

21. Kinross, P., *Atatürk: The Rebirth of a Nation* (London: Weidenfeld and Nicolson, 2012), p. 100.

22. Allen and Muratoff, *Caucasian Battlefields, A History of Wars on the Turco-Caucasian Border, 1828-1921*, p.422.

23. Ibid., p.428.

24. Ibid.

25. Erickson, *Ordered to Die: A History of the Ottoman Army in the First World War*, p.119.

26. Ibid., p.120.

27. Liman von Sanders, *Five Years in Turkey*, p.190.

Chapter 5: Die Fliegertruppe

1. Mahoney and Pugh, 'Air Warfare'.

2. Wells, M., 'Aircraft, Fighter and Pursuit', *International Encyclopedia of First World War Studies* [Online], 2016. URL: https://encyclopedia.1914-1918-online.net/article/aircraft_fighter_and_pursuit

3. Storey, W.K., *The First World War: A Concise Global History* (Plymouth: Rowman & Littlefield Publishers, Inc., 2009), p.130.

4. Sterling, C.H., 'Fokker Aircraft (Early Years, World War I)', in W.J. Boyne (ed.), *Air Warfare: An International Encyclopedia: A–L* (Oxford: ABC-CLIO, 2002), p.227.

5. Head, R. G., *Oswald Boelcke: Germany's First Fighter Ace and Father of Air Combat* (London: Grub Street, 2016), p.104.

6. Mahoney and Pugh, 'Air Warfare'.

7. Burg and Purcell, *Almanac of World War I*, p.114.

8. Murphy, J.D., *Military Aircraft, Origins to 1918: An Illustrated History of Their Impact* (Oxford: ABC-CLIO, 2005), p.57.

9. Miller, R., *Trenchard: Father of the Royal Air Force* (London: Weidenfeld and Nicolson, 2017), p.95.

10. Ibid.

11. See, Head, *Oswald Boelcke: Germany's First Fighter Ace and Father of Air Combat*, p.105; Murphy, *Military Aircraft, Origins to 1918: An Illustrated History of Their Impact*, p.57.

12. Ibid., p.106.

13. Dowling, *The Brusilov Offensive*, p.145.

14. Knox, A.W.F., *With the Russian Army, 1914–1917, Vol. II* (London: Hutchinson & Co, 1921), p.118.

15. Williams, A.G. and Gustin, E., *Flying Guns of World War I: Development of Aircraft Guns, Ammunition and Installations 1914–32* (Crawley: Airlife, 2004), p.80.

16. Black, J., *Air Power: A Global History* (Maryland: The Rowman & Littlefield Publishing Group, Inc, 2016), p.28.

17. Atrash, N., 'Mapping Palestine: The Bavarian Air Force WWI Aerial Photography', *Jerusalem Quarterly*, 56 (1) 2014, p.96.

18. Erickson, *Gallipoli & the Middle East 1914–1918: From the Dardanelles to Mesopotamia*, p.78.

19. Erickson, *Ordered to Die. A History of the Ottoman Army in the First World War*, p.228–229.

20. Nicolle, D., *The Ottoman Army 1914-1918* (Oxford: Osprey, 1994), p.9.

21. Knight, P., *The British Army in Mesopotamia, 1914-1918* (London: McFarland & Company, Inc., Publishers, 2013), p.73.

22. Mahoney and Pugh, 'Air Warfare'.

23. Geinitz, C., 'Strategic Bombing of German Cities', in R. Chickering and S. Förster (eds.), *Great War, Total War: Combat and Mobilization on the Western Front, 1914-1918* (Cambridge: Cambridge University Press, 2000), p.212.

24. Raleigh, W.A., *The War in the Air: Being the Story of the Part Played in the Great War by the Royal Air Force, Volume 6* (Oxford: Clarendon Press, 1937), p.119.

25. *The Times*, 5th February 1916, The British Library, London (BL), p.7.

26. *The Times*, 'Bishop of London and the Skipper', 7th February 1916, The British Library, London (BL), p.10.
27. Corum, J.S. and Muller, R.R., 'Instructions on the Mission and Utilization of Flying Units within the Army', in J. S. Corum and R. R. Muller (eds.), *The Luftwaffe's Way of War. German Air Doctrine, 1911–1945* (Baltimore, MD: Nautical & *Aviation* Publishing, 1998), p.62.
28. Baker, L. and Cooling, B.F., 'Developments and Lessons Before World War II', in B. F. Cooling (eds.), *Case Studies in the Achievement of Air Superiority* (Washington: Air Force History and Museums Program, 1994), p. 3.
29. Vanwyngarden, G., *Albatros Aces of World War I Part 2: Aircraft of the Aces No. 77* (Oxford: Osprey Publishing, 2007), p.19.

Chapter 6: Kaiserliche Marine

1. Rasor, E., *The Battle of Jutland. A Bibliography* (Westport, CT: Greenwood Press, 1992), pp.63–170.
2. Brooks, J., *The Battle of Jutland* (Cambridge: Cambridge University Press, 2016), pp.140–142.
3. Gröner, E., Jung, D. and Maass, M., *U-boats and Mine Warfare Vessels. German Warships 1815–1945* (London: Conway Maritime Press, 1991), p.6.
4. Gray, E., *Captains Of War: They Fought Beneath the Sea* (London: Leo Cooper Ltd, 1988), p.137.
5. Tarrant, V. E., *Jutland: The German Perspective: A New View of the Great Battle, 31 May 1916* (London: Arms & Armour Press, 1995), pp.65–66.
6. Rahn, W., 'The Battle of Jutland from the German perspective', in M. Epkenhans, J. Hillmann, F. Nägler (eds.), *Jutland: World War I's Greatest Naval Battle* (Lexington: The University Press of Kentucky, 2015), p.156.
7. Canwell, D. and Sutherland, J., *The Battle of Jutland* (Barnsley: Pen & Sword Maritime, 2007), p.138.
8. Campbell, J., *Jutland: An Analysis of the Fighting* (Guildford: Lyons Press, 1998), p.31.
9. Stille, M., *British Battlecruiser vs German Battlecruiser: 1914–16* (Oxford: Osprey Publishing, 2013), p.178.
10. Ibid., pp.178–179.
11. David, D., *1916: Verdun to the Somme: Key Dates and Events from the Third Year of the First World War* (London: Hodder & Stoughton, 2013), p.57.
12. Tarrant, *Jutland: The German Perspective: A New View of the Great Battle, 31 May 1916*, p.259.
13. *Daily Mirror*, 'The Battle of Jutland', 3rd June 1916, The British Library, London (BL).
14. Osborne, R., *The Battle of Jutland: History's Greatest Sea Battle Told Through Newspaper Reports, Official Documents and the Accounts of Those Who Were There* (Barnsley: Pen & Sword Books Ltd, 2016), p.125.

15. Osborne, *The Battle of Jutland: History's Greatest Sea Battle Told Through Newspaper Reports, Official Documents and the Accounts of Those Who Were There*, p.126.
16. Hillmann, J., 'Remembering the Battle of Jutland in Germany', in M. Epkenhans, J. Hillmann and F. Nägler (eds.), *Jutland: World War I's Greatest Naval Battle* (Lexington: The University Press of Kentucky, 2015), p.311.
17. Osborne, *The Battle of Jutland: History's Greatest Sea Battle Told Through Newspaper Reports, Official Documents and the Accounts of Those Who Were There*, p.127.
18. Vego, M.N., *Naval Strategy and Operations in Narrow Seas* (Abingdon: Frank Cass Publishers, 2003), p.168.
19. Burg, Almanac of World War I, p.221.
20. Tucker, *World War I: A Student Encyclopedia*, p.589.
21. Ferguson, N., *The Pity of War* (London: Penguin Books, 1999), p.283.

Chapter 7: Heim Front
1. Fallada, H., *Little Man, What Now?* (London: Melville House Publishing, 2009).
2. Allen, K., 'Sharing Scarcity: Bread Rationing and the First World War in Berlin, 1914-1923', *Journal of Social History*, 32 (2) 1998, pp.371–393.
3. Herwig, *The First World War: Germany and Austro-Hungary 1914–1918*, p.291.
4. Ibid., p.272.
5. Loewenberg, P.P., 'Germany, The Home Front (I): The Physical and Psychological Consequences of Home Front Hardship', in H. Cecil and P. Liddle (eds.), *Facing Armageddon: The First World War Experience* (London: Leo Cooper, 1996), p.556.
6. Watson, *Ring of Steel: Germany and Austria-Hungary at War, 1914-1918*, p.117.
7. Loewenberg, 'Germany, The Home Front (I): The Physical and Psychological Consequences of Home Front Hardship', p.556.
8. Jackson, A., 'Germany, The Home Front (2): Blockade, Government and Revolution', in H. Cecil and P. Liddle (eds.), *Facing Armageddon: The First World War Experience* (London: Leo Cooper, 1996), p.571.
9. Herwig, *The First World War: Germany and Austro-Hungary 1914–1918*, p.275.
10. Watson, *Ring of Steel: Germany and Austria-Hungary at War, 1914-1918*, p.119.
11. Davis, B., 'Food and Nutrition (Germany)', *International Encyclopedia for First World War Studies* [Online], 2014. URL: https://encyclopedia.1914-1918-online.net/article/food_and_nutrition_germany
12. Herwig, *The First World War: Germany and Austro-Hungary 1914–1918*, pp.225–226.
13. Ibid., p.225.
14. Watson, *Ring of Steel: Germany and Austria-Hungary at War, 1914-1918*, p.114.
15. Fritzsche, P., *Germans into Nazis* (London: Harvard University Press, 2000), p.68.